T0069268

THE NAGASAKI PEACE DISCOURSE

The Nagasaki Peace Discourse: City Hall and the Quest for a Nuclear Free World

Geoffrey C. Gunn

*The Nagasaki Peace Discourse: City Hall and
the Quest for a Nuclear Free World*
Geoffrey C. Gunn
NIAS Asia Briefings series

First published in 2019 by NIAS Press
NIAS – Nordic Institute of Asian Studies
Øster Farimagsgade 5, 1353 Copenhagen K, Denmark
Tel.: +45 3532 9503 • Fax: +45 3532 9549
E-mail: books@nias.ku.dk • Online: www.niaspress.dk

© Geoffrey G. Gunn 2019
No material may be reproduced in whole or in part
without the express permission of the publisher

British Library Cataloguing in Publication Data
A CIP record for this book is available from the British Library

ISBN: 978-87-7694-274-8 (pbk)
ISBN: 978-87-7694-690-6 (e-book)

Typesetting by Donald B. Wagner
Printed and bound in the United States
by Maple Press, York, PA

Contents

Preface

Writing on the 73rd anniversary of the dropping of atomic bombs on Hiroshima and Nagasaki, myself a 20-year resident in Nagasaki, I admit to only a somewhat belated engagement with local nuclear politics. Anointed 'professor of international relations' in the faculty of economics of Nagasaki University, I expected to be plunged into local peace politics. How wrong I was. Academic culture, language and even tribalism threw up insuperable barriers. It is also understood that even Japanese who have settled in Nagasaki from other prefectures have difficulty in adjusting to the local dialect and ways. Still, I found that local Catholics, the bishop included, were internationally engaged at a number of levels, as with future outcomes of then Indonesian-occupied East Timor, an interest I also shared.

Nestled behind Nishiyama or West Mountain, the Meiji-era red brick campus of my faculty emerged unscathed from the atomic bombing. Not so the medical faculty sited close to the hypocentre, incinerated in the bombing and duly memorialized. Nevertheless, as I learned, the ancient towering camphor trees on my campus had their branches sheared off and the precinct and its population was subject to fallout in the form of 'black rain' in the aftermath of the bombing. While I strove to inject some element of peace discourse into my lectures, many of the students arriving from beyond Nagasaki Prefecture appeared to have little knowledge of the city, its rich and layered history as the first point of contact in Japan between arriving Portuguese and Dutch in the late sixteenth and early seventeenth centuries, the international context of the war, much less awareness of local controversies surrounding nuclear politics. As I also learned, probably fewer than half of students had even bothered to visit the atomic bomb museum. While some of the faculty did engage issues of war and peace, they also retreated into the world of academic specialisms or adopted bureaucratic personas, to put it politely.

As an aside that is really more than aside, this tendency to treat disaster as a private matter and national disaster as a national private matter extends well beyond Nagasaki. The lesson was recently re-taught to the many foreign journalists who arrived to report on the Fukushima nuclear disaster.

Egged on by American occupation bureaucrats, hastily recreated post-war national universities, as in Nagasaki, were harnessed to science and mathematical literacy in the effort to rebuild the nation. Social issues and debate were relegated to the margins. Up to this day, Nagasaki University lacks a social science faculty or even department. Together, computer-graded university entrance exams and the school curriculum famously contrive to narrow student knowledge of Japan's wartime history, much less its broader interna-tional context. By contrast, or so it would seem, young adults become socialized into national politics via pulp and now digital media with its heterodox and often seductive neo-nationalist claims frequently contrary to the facts. Still, primary school children in Nagasaki (and Hiroshima) are routinely called upon to show their faces at anniversary events associated with the bombings, flanked by parents and other citizens in moving and genuine displays of reverence.

Still, I thank those among my Nagasaki students who dared to share their private views in written essays (but hardly ever publicly). I also thank Chieko and Kenji as my primary interpreters and/or translators. I thank Craig Collie and/or his publisher for sending me a copy of his book, *Nagasaki*. I thank contributors and editors of *Asia Pacific/Japan Focus* for helping me to interpret contemporary Japanese politics, including the Fukushima atomic power plant meltdown disaster. I also thank two anonymous reviewers for further guidance as well as a NIAS Press text editor. Note that I have adopted Japanese naming conventions as with writing family names first.

Abbreviations

CNIC	Citizen's Nuclear Information Center
CTBT	Comprehensive Nuclear Test Ban Treaty
ECOSOC	Economic and Social Affairs Council
FCNA	Forum for Nuclear Cooperation in Asia
Gensuiko	The Japan Council against Atomic and Hydrogen Bombs
GHQ	General Headquarters
ICAN	The International Campaign to Abolish Nuclear Weapons
JAEC	Japan Atomic Energy Commission
JCP	Japan Communist Party
JINED	International Nuclear Energy Development of Japan
JSP	Japan Socialist Party
LDP	Liberal Democratic Party
NAA	National Archives of Australia
NEA-NWFZ	Northeast Asia Nuclear Weapons-Free Zone
NHK	Japan Broadcasting Corporation
NPT	Nuclear Non-Proliferation of Nuclear Weapons
NRA	Nuclear Regulation Authority
POW	Prisoner of War

RECNA	Research Center for Nuclear Weapons Abolition
SCAP	Supreme Commander for the Allied Powers
SDF	Self-Defense Forces
UK	United Kingdom
UNESCO	United Nations
US	United States
USIS	US Information Service
USSR	Union of Soviet Socialist Republics

Introduction: Drawing the Parameters of the Japanese Nuclear Debate

F or some it is enough to stand, pause, and maybe pray at the space in Nagasaki today memorialized by an obelisk placed at the hypocentre above which the 'Fat Man' bomb detonated at 11:02 local time on 9 August 1945. Coming three days after the A-bombing of Hiroshima, the even more powerful plutonium bomb dropped over Nagasaki's northern Urakami district. As George LeRoy reports, this created a nuclear chain reaction that would release the energy of about 21 kilotons of TNT dynamite, incinerated the landscape and instantly killed an estimated 20,000 people, an additional 20,000 or more succumbing to radiation poisoning and other illnesses within the week. Taking into account those who would subsequently succumb from to their wounds or radiation-linked cancer and other diseases, the total death count is now conventionally rounded to 74,000. Nagasaki was then a city of some 240,000 (among them 9,000 Japanese soldiers, 10–12,000 Koreans and many hundreds of Chinese conscripts and Allied POWs). The contrast between the devastation of 9 August 1945 and present-day Nagasaki could not be greater; it is now a bustling modern city of around 430,000 and with background radiation at about normal for any place on earth.

You have made the pilgrimage, you have visited the Atomic Bomb Museum and, over several hours, you have drunk deeply on the history, the science, the awesome destructive power of the bomb dropped on Nagasaki and the anti-nuclear weapons peace message that comes through strongly. Perhaps you have mentally registered the official Japanese 'peace discourse'. Alone among nations, and a gift of the five-year American occupation of the country, Japan has a war-renouncing constitution. Going one step further, in 1971 Japan embraced the three so-called non-nuclear principles; namely, renouncing the possession, production, and introduction of nuclear weapons into Japanese territory. You may have preconceived ideas on the linkage between the bombs and Japan's surrender announced six days after the bombing of Nagasaki, but can you now identify with the victims and those who still suffer? And can you ask yourself: should use of this terrible weapon of mass destruction ever again be contemplated in any circumstances?

Known as *hibakusha* (literally 'explosion-affected people'), few direct victims or sufferers are with us today. With most of them octogenarians or older, this book departs from pre-cursors that have sought to capture the words of the victims through direct interviews.[1] Nevertheless, together with their *nissei* or second generation descendants, they have come to symbolize the suffering of ordinary people as victims of this

---

1   The Nagasaki National Peace Memorial Hall for the Atomic Bomb Victims has compiled and archived many hundreds of oral histories of atomic bomb survivors. Samples have been translated into English. See Brian Burke-Gaffney, *Nagasaki Speaks: A Record of the Atomic Bombing* (The Nagasaki International Culture Hall, 1993). For possibly the most comprehensive bibliography of hibakusha sources, see Susan Southard, *Nagasaki: Life after Nuclear War* (New York: Viking, 2015, 349–72), in turn one of the more recent works on Nagasaki to work within this genre.

weapon of mass destruction, and are even acknowledged in United Nations declarations. As will become clear in the telling of this story, the meaning of *hibakusha* has been contested from the beginning. First came questions about which individuals truly qualified for the status (and benefits) that accrued to true *Hibakusha*. Next, some sought to release the concept from its narrow Hiroshima-Nagasaki origins and use it as a symbol of a nuclear free-world, as for example with the 1970s–80s slogan, 'No! More! Hibakusha!' More recently, with Three Mile Island and Chernobyl still living memories, fears that followed the 2011 Fukushima disaster led to the power of the *hibakusha* legacy, namely removing the specter of all forms of nuclear death from the future of mankind.

You, the reader, might wonder what else you don't know about Japan's modern history: its slide into militarism, its war of aggression in China extending into Southeast Asia and the Pacific, US wartime bombing of practically all Japanese cities, and the post-war Allied occupation and makeover of Japan along with war crimes trials? You might also marvel at Japan's rebirth as a US Cold War ally, its embrace of a 'peace' constitution, its post-war economic rise from the ashes and its generous contributions to international order. But again you ponder the nation's conversion to civilian use of nuclear power notwithstanding the seismic and other risks, as exemplified by the triple meltdown of the Fukushima nuclear power plant on 11 March 2011 in the throes of a natural disaster. Emotions, preconceptions and intellect are called into play.

Millions of words have been written on the atomic bombings, but mine is a Nagasaki narrative written at a juncture when the city seeks to further inscribe or make the memory of the 9 August 1945 tragedy indelible. This comes at a time when the number of those with direct memories of the bombing is dwindling. Moreover, in an age when the spectre of nuclear war over the Korean Peninsula has again been raised, the second and last atomic-bombed city on the planet seeks to serve a stern and sombre warning to the world.

And yet, we are also witnessing a political juncture in Japan where voices calling for the scrapping of the nation's sacred 'peace constitution' have become increasingly strident and where even the truth about the Fukushima meltdown disaster continues to be hostage to the 'nuclear village' or the nation's powerful pro-nuclear business-industrial-political elites. The paradox of an atomic-bombed city living under the shadow of the American nuclear umbrella is also stark, with Nagasaki Prefecture itself host to US nuclear-powered warships and, we can believe, even nuclear weapons. To be sure, the award of the 2017 Nobel Peace Prize to a group opposing nuclear weapons (The International Campaign to Abolish Nuclear Weapons, ICAN) was well received in Nagasaki and Hiroshima, especially in a year when the threat of nuclear warfare also touching Japan seemed to have drawn closer.

Drawing the Parameters of the Japanese Nuclear Debate

Although possession of nuclear weapons is not forbidden by the Japanese constitution, Japan has repeatedly expressed its abhorrence of nuclear arms early on and determined never to acquire them. As the only nation to experience the devastation of atomic attack, it claims the right to speak forthrightly about the devastation such weapons can bring and have brought. The Basic Atomic Energy Law of 1956 limits research, development and utilization of nuclear power to peaceful uses and, as mentioned, national policy has embodied 'three non-nuclear principles: forbidding the nation to possess or manufacture nuclear weapons or to allow them to be introduced into the nation. The notion was formalized by the Japanese Diet or parliament on 24 November 1971. In 1976 Japan ratified the Nuclear Non-Proliferation Treaty (NPT), adopted by the UN Security Council in 1968, and reiterated its intention never to 'develop, use, or allow the transportation of nuclear weapons through its territory.' Japan became a signatory to the Comprehensive Nuclear-Test-Ban Treaty (CTBT) in 1997 and has actively worked towards strengthening non-proliferation and disarmament regimes.

Paradoxically, as discussed below, even as a victim of nuclear holocaust, Japan embraced civilian nuclear power. Lacking significant domestic sources of energy except for coal, Japan must import substantial amounts of crude oil, natural gas and other energy resources. That came to include uranium and with Japan's nuclear output nearly doubling between 1985 and 1996, as the nation attempted to move away from dependence on oil following the 1973 Arab oil embargo. In recent years, the nuclear industry has promoted itself as rising to the challenges posed by global climate change. As of 2000, Japan ranked third worldwide in installed nuclear capacity, behind the United States and France. Japan's nuclear technology and ambiguous nuclear inclinations have provided a considerable nuclear potential, becoming a virtual or 'paranuclear' state.

History has proved that Japan's embrace of nuclear energy has offered a poisoned chalice.

In their edited volume on nuclear debates in Asia, Mike Mochizuki and Deepa Ollapally observe that domestic debates are structured along what they term Nationalist, Realist and Globalist schools of thought, a taxonomy that invites analysis of how domestic political configurations affect Japan's nuclear policies alongside those of such other Asian nations as India, Pakistan, China, South Korea, Vietnam and Taiwan. Insodoing they challenge dominant neo-realist thinking, which holds that nuclear policy is a by-product of competition in the international system, and so offer a counterpoint to conventional security studies approaches. In line with the general Mochizuki and Ollapally thesis, this book argues that the tension and sometimes clash between (Nagasaki) globalists and (Tokyo) realists and nationalists is quite apparent. Remembrance, the struggle for recognition on the part of surviving victims or *hibakusha*, and the no less earnest struggle waged by City Hall in Nagasaki to bring to world attention the threat of nuclear weapons, defines the globalist perspective or what I term here as the Nagasaki peace discourse. Essentially the realists welcome the nuclear umbrella provided by the US–Japan Treaty system and have eagerly embraced civilian nuclear power under the 'atoms-for-peace' slogan. For their part, the nationalists perceive Japan's 'peace constitution' as rife for revision as they look ahead to a 'normal' Japan implying a legal Self-Defense Force or Army as an instrument in international relations as in peacekeeping operations and, for some, even a nuclear-armed Japan.

Beneath the surface, as in Japan at large, civil society in Nagasaki is highly lively, as with Catholic and Protestant churches, social clubs, NGOs, trade unions, Rotary Clubs and the like, political parties including a communist party (which runs a virtually free clinic in my current neighbourhood). Likewise, municipal elections for Nagasaki's City Hall, gubernatorial elections at the prefectural level and national elections are ritualistic and, in Nagasaki, a conservative city both socially and politically with it characteristic annual calendar of Shintoist, Buddhist and Catholic rituals and ceremonies, the ruling Liberal Democratic Party (LDP) or its proxies sweep virtually every election. But that is not to say that the Nagasaki City Hall lacks outreach. The reverse is the case and, laudably, the city authorities strive to connect with a global audience not only to win attention to their victimhood but to spread the anti-nuclear proliferation message. Even so, as this work elaborates, City Hall has frequently been a site of contestation between mayors of conscience (at least one of them Catholic), nationalist or war revisionist opinion, political pressure exerted by Tokyo and even brutal handling by local *yakuza* crime syndicates.

With such civil society activity in mind, an opening chapter in the book first illustrates Nagasaki's unique-in-Japan Christian origins as well as drawing a portrait of the pre-war city and its early post-war revival under American auspices. A second chapter focuses on the revelation of the atomic bombing by the first arriving journalists and their struggle against American censorship as a global anti-nuclear movement began to take form. A third chapter traces the origins of a peace discourse as it emerged locally in Nagasaki especially around a Catholic figure and, during a later period, among survivors also adding their voices for recognition and compensation. A fourth chapter describes the Allied POW experience and narrative, important voices as many of the survivor-victims lived into long age. A fifth chapter highlights Nagasaki (and its Peace Park) as an enduring symbol of global peace movements, variously Soviet-inspired or stemming from China's memory of Japan's aggressive war and/or part of the burgeoning global anti-nuclear sentiment. Chapter 6 focuses upon the way that the tragedy has been remembered and memorialized with especial reference to Nagasaki's Atomic Bomb Museum. A seventh chapter brings to the fore what I describe as the Nagasaki City Hall peace discourse, or the anti-nuclear proliferation politics for which the respective city mayors have added their names and sober message. Chapter 8 seeks to especially capture the national debate on civilian nuclear power in the wake of the Fukushima nuclear power plant disaster of March 2011. A final reflection seeks to invoke the mood in Nagasaki today.

Chapter 1

Nagasaki: The Historical Setting

L ooking back at Nagasaki's origins, as many have remarked, the irony of US war planners targeting Japan's largest Christian community recalls the language of US President Barack Obama during his March 2016 visit to Hiroshima on 'difficult history'. First touched by Christian missionaries in 1568 arriving from Macau with Portuguese traders, the city owed its origins as an international port to the decision of the local *daimyo* (feudal lord) of Omura to grant Nagasaki to the Jesuits. As church histories reveal, over the following decades arriving missionaries were amazingly successful in winning converts to Christianity in and outside Nagasaki. Besides the erection of a Jesuit seminary, numerous other churches were constructed around the town and with Franciscan, Dominican and Augustinian missionaries vying with each other to win converts and influence, not excluding numerous daimyo, their retainers and peasant masses alike. Nevertheless, with the tide turning against Christianity and with the promulgation of exclusion edicts and the persecution of Catholic missionaries and converts, culminating with the final expulsion of Iberians c.1635, the 'Christian century' in Nagasaki came to an end.[1]

---

1 The best source on this history in the English language remains the classic works of historian Charles Boxer. I have summarized much of this literature in my *World Trade Systems of the East and West: Nagasaki and the Asian Bullion Trade Networks* (Brill: Leiden, 2018), Chap. 2.

Practically nothing tangible remains of this history but it has been imaginatively captured in *Silence*, the 1966 novel by Japanese writer Endo Shusaku and, in turn, the derivative 2016 American historical drama film of the same name directed by Martin Scorsese. Having been deliberately destroyed in successive waves of anti-Christian persecution back in the early seventeenth century, it is salutary that the site of one such church, that of São Domingos, became the object of an impressive archaeological excavation and preservation exercise, at the end of the last century revealing structural remains and a large number of artefacts linked with the former church.

Still, following the expulsion of the Portuguese, a Western presence continued in Nagasaki as the Protestant Dutch gained exclusive sanction to maintain a trading post right inside Nagasaki harbour on an artificial island named Deshima, (the stone remnants of which survived the atomic bombing and which today is a well-visited tourist site that showcases this period of Nagasaki's history). In fact the Dutch inheritance came to surpass the Portuguese, especially in the transmission of Western medicine, science and technology, and this is remembered and also memorialized (as with tracing back the origins of Nagasaki University's medical school to the pioneering work of Dutch surgeon Pompe van Meerdervoort who initiated medical lectures in the Dutch language in November 1857, going on to set up a medical school).

Simply put, Nagasaki was Tokugawa Japan's window on the western world for over 250 years. Undoubtedly the virtual extraterritorial rule enjoyed by the Jesuits and Portuguese traders at Nagasaki was unique in Japanese history although, it might be added, there were pale echoes with the creation of foreign 'settlements' or enclaves in the late nineteenth century following Commodore Mathew Perry's famous 'opening' of Japan, as in Nagasaki, Yokohama and, indeed, as with American military bases in Japan until the present.[2]

The arrival in 1863 of missionaries of the Paris-based Société des Missions Etrangères also proved epochal, especially in the way of making contact with Christian believers of a surviving underground Christian tradition still prevalent on offshore islands as well as inside Nagasaki at Urakami (site of the Catholic cathedral razed by the atomic bombing). Still under the threat of severe official sanction, the ban of Christianity was officially lifted in 1873 and Catholic Christians maintained a strong presence in the Urakami quarter at the time of the atomic bombing. Christian voices were especially strong in Nagasaki in the decades following the bombing, carried through by Motoshima Hitoshi, himself a Catholic who served four terms as mayor of Nagasaki, from 1979 to 1995. Even today, Nagasaki Prefecture hosts the largest number of Catholics in Japan. In 2016 the still extant Oura church, erected in 1864 by the French mission in a more secluded part of the city, was awarded minor basilica status by the Vatican. It was here that 'hidden' Christians or those who kept alive a Christian tradition dating back to the persecutions of the seventeenth century first revealed themselves to church authorities in the form of a march from

---

2   I have greatly elaborated upon Nagasaki's role in servicing Japan's silk-for-silver trade in my *World Trade Systems of the East and West*, Chaps 3, 4, 6.

Urakami. Two years later, the church along with 12 other memory sites scattered through neighbouring islands was awarded world heritage status.

Nagasaki's Pioneer Role in Japan's Industrialization

Another feature of Nagasaki's modern history is that it served as a crucible for Japan's early modernization, and its fine harbour remained an asset over the centuries. Meiji-era industrialization was even anticipated locally by the Tokugawa Shogunate. Notably, a group of Dutch engineers were commissioned in 1857 to construct a foundry for the purpose of building large ships, including naval vessels, and the task was completed in 1862. Then followed the opening of Japan's first steam-powered dock in December 1868. With the advent of Meiji in the same year, both the foundry complex and dock were purchased by the new government and passed to the Mitsubishi conglomerate between 1884 and 1887. A key player in Nagasaki's success was the Scottish arms dealer and merchant-innovator, Thomas Glover (celebrated locally today in the form of a theme park), who introduced Japan's first mechanized steam power pumps in the Takashima coal mines, purchased outright by Mitsubishi in 1881. Six years later Mitsubishi took over the Hashima undersea coal mines on an offshore island, infamously worked with slave labour from China and Korea during World War II and closing only in 1974, when the coal reserves were nearing depletion. Also known as Gunkanjima or 'battleship island,' Hashima is becoming more widely recognized as part of Japan's 'dark heritage,' as some of these wartime sites are now known.

As observed by Brian Burke-Gaffney, a historian of Nagasaki's modernization, with the establishment of the Nagasaki Shipyard and Machinery Works in 1857, Mitsubishi's fortunes in shipping began to boom, just as Japan's 'Taiwan Expedition' of 1874 was basically launched from Nagasaki. Foreign advisers assisted Mitsubishi's establishment of its own dry dock between 1901 and 1905, and the company imported a massive cantilever crane from Scotland in 1909 (both are still in operation over one hundred years later). By around 1870, Kobe and Yokohama would eclipse Nagasaki as an international business centre, and Meiji Japan's iron and steel industry began to take a different direction. Nevertheless, Mitsubishi maintained its stake in shipbuilding and heavy engineering in Nagasaki, going on in 1942 to deliver the largest warship ever built: the (ill-fated) 76,000 tonne *Musashi*. At the same time it also operated weapons plants north of the harbour and located closer to the atomic bomb epicentre.

Proximity to Shanghai helped Nagasaki's early modernization as well. Connected to Shanghai by telegraph in August 1871, another first for Japan, Nagasaki emerged as a European capitalist appendage upon an even larger economic base on the eastern seaboard of China.

Even prior to Meiji, the British along with Americans, French, Russians, Prussians and other nationalities, carved out a 'foreign settlement' in Nagasaki. This came effective on 1 July 1859, and with Japan hosting seven foreign settlements by 1899 at least until the system of extraterritorial privileges was abolished in that year. Non-Japanese residents, including nationals of neutral nations, would flee the 'foreign settlement' in Nagasaki by way of 'exchange ships' on the eve of the attack on Pearl Harbor. Practically none would return, and but few relics of the settlement would survive the atomic bombing and/or post-war demolition. One that did survive is the former Hong Kong & Shanghai Bank, a solid stone fortress turned into military police headquarters during the war.

Nagasaki as a Wartime Target

All told, the northern Urakami factory district comprised some 100 small and medium size workshops cooperating with Mitsubishi in a zone stretching from mid-Urakami to the estuary entering Nagasaki Harbour.[3] Notwithstanding Nagasaki's wartime role, as with the construction of the *Musashi* and in the production of munitions and missiles, compared to Hiroshima's heavy industrial complex and army and naval bases, or even the Kokura heavy industrial complex in what is now known as Kitakyushu and the original priority target for the second atomic bombing, it was a relatively minor target in August 1945. As many have commented, the mid-1945 the atomic destruction of Nagasaki had only a negligible impact upon Japan's capacity to wage further war.

Fatefully, as discussed at an initial meeting of the 'Target Committee' of 27 April 1945, Nagasaki was placed on a US

---

3   *Nagasaki National Peace Memorial Hall for the Atomic Bomb Victims: The Nagasaki Atomic Bomb Damage Records*, Part 1, Chap. 2.

shortlist of potential target cities (Tokyo Bay, Kawasaki, Yokohama, Nagoya, Osaka, Kobe, Kyoto, Hiroshima, Kure, Yawata, Kokura, Shimonoseki, Yamaguchi, Kumamoto, Fukuoka, Sasebo).[4] Subsequent 'target committee' meetings narrowed the short list and Nagasaki emerged as one of four possible targets (along with Hiroshima, Kokura and Niigata) reserved, in the words of historian Mark Selden, 'to display the awesome power of the atom to Japan and the world'. These words bear even further reflection when we recall that the target for the atomic bomb over Nagasaki was not the northern Urakami factory district but the even more populous historical city further to the south.

Post-war Nagasaki

With its magnificent natural harbour and its shipbuilding industry locally pioneered by Mitsubishi, Nagasaki was obviously never innocent of wartime activities and, indeed, like other Japanese port cities, was a hub of activity. Nagasaki is still known as a Mitsubishi town, and still retains its original harbourside real estate along with other wartime industrial sites. Having weathered the early post-war dismantling of wartime *zaibatsu* or conglomerates, as demanded by GHQ (General Headquarters) of the Supreme Commander for the

---

4 Anon, Notes on Initial Meeting of Target Committee, 2 May 1945, Source: RG 77, MED Records, Top Secret Documents, File no. 5d (copy from microfilm). See also *The Nagasaki Atomic Bomb Damage Records: General Analysis Version,* Vol. I (revised version) (Nagasaki City, 2016, 65–70) which reproduces the 'Atomic Bombing Order' or letter from General Thomas Handy, Acting Chief of Staff, to General Carl Spaatz of the US Army Strategic Air Force, authorizing the dropping of the first atomic bomb.

Allied Powers (SCAP), the advent of the Korean War in 1951 in tandem with SCAP supremo Douglas MacArthur's policy reversal with respect to the elimination of war criminals and war-complicit industrial combines granted Mitsubishi a new lease on life.

The industrial behemoth also helped refuel Nagasaki's post-bomb reconstruction, with its harbour and ship works once again coming into play. Post-war Mitsubishi re-established Japan's shipping industry, going on into the 1990s to produce high-end cruise ships. The Mitsubishi Nagasaki Shipping Company also built the first Japanese-made US-modelled Aegis warship for the Japanese Maritime Self-Defense Force (SDF) launched in 1991. In addition, Urakami is still home to Japan's only torpedo-producing factory. Mitsubishi/Nagasaki thus stands out as one of the major beneficiaries of collaborative US–Japanese efforts to produce weapons *and* to introduce nuclear energy into the country.

Nagasaki Prefecture hosts the third largest American military base in Japan today. In 1946 the US took over the Japanese imperial naval base in Sasebo, located just 68 kilometres from Nagasaki city. During the Korean War, Sasebo was reorganized by the US into a military port that housed a headquarters of the United Nations Forces. Nagasaki Airport also served the US military base in Sasebo as a point of entry into and exit from Japan. Under the Japan–US Security Treaty of 8 September 1951, Japan was obliged to offer base facilities to the US while, reciprocally, prohibiting Japan from providing other foreign powers any bases or military-related rights without US consent.

The Korean War also offered employment to some locals, as with my informant 'Johnny' who described to me in rare, grammatically elegant English how he had followed this kind of career. Not a *hibakusha*, having been removed at a young age from his family-run plantation in northern Sumatra just prior to Japan's invasion of what was then the Dutch East Indies, he survived the war in the Tatura internee camp for Japanese in Victoria, Australia. At war's end, he was unceremoniously returned to Japan, making his way home to a devastated city he had hardly known. With his obvious bilingual skills then in high-demand, he quickly ingratiated himself with American occupiers and went on to work as a civilian employee on US projects in Nagasaki Prefecture and then in Korea.[5] No doubt such an interrogation feeds into the myriad life histories of *hibakusha* and others who lived out their lives in the difficult early decades following the dropping of the atomic bomb. With its industrial base and large working class population, the relative decline of the local shipbuilding industry also led to some diversification and with tourism emerging as a major economic prop to the local economy. In Chapter 3 we shall explain how City Hall sought to reinvent Nagasaki as a city of international culture in part to promote the city's physical recovery from nuclear destruction, but also to showcase its unique history.

---

5   Johnny was repatriated from Australia along with 2,562 compatriots on the *Koei Maru*, arriving at Uraga port on 13 March 1946. By all accounts a wrenching voyage through tropical seas, the arrivals faced severe challenges. According to Yuriko Nagata, 'Japanese Internment in Australia during World War II' (Ph.D. thesis submitted to Adelaide University, September 1993, pp.264–65), more than a few of the Indonesia-born or connected Japanese returnees from Australian internment camps found work on American bases, putting their English skill to advantage.

Chapter 2

The Anti-Nuclear Discourse Takes Form: First Exposure and American Censorship

Nicknamed Fat Man by the Americans, the bomb dropped on Nagasaki on 9 August 1945 was an implosion-type nuclear weapon with a solid plutonium core (a cutaway model is on display in Nagasaki's Atomic Bomb Museum). It was carried by the B-29 plane Bockscar, flown from Tinian in the Mariana Islands and piloted by Maj. Gen. Charles Sweeney. Dropped by parachute, the bomb containing a core of about 6.4 kilograms of plutonium exploded at precisely 11:02 approximately 500 metres above ground over Urakami or 3.4 kilometres northwest of the planned target: the heart of the historical city. As a result, the direct blast was confined to the Urakami Valley. Unlike Hiroshima, a major portion of the city was protected by the intervening hills. As with the Hiroshima bomb, the major effect of the Fat Man bomb on Nagasaki was an extreme heat and pressure blast accompanied by a strong burst of gamma radiation and a more limited burst of neutrons. People were exposed to the combined heat and radiation blasts. All three were deadly to humans. Most people located within 1.5 km of the hypocenter were killed, and fires destroyed most wooden structures in the neighbourhoods girding the harbour, including the historic Centre. Fallout in the form of 'black rain' contaminated most of the population even beyond the Urakami Valley in the following days.

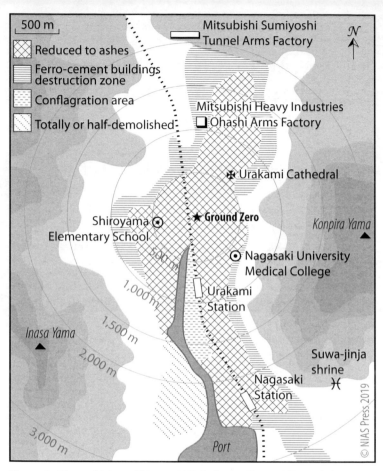

Figure 1. General Map of Nagasaki Relative to Ground Zero, 9 August 1945. (Source: adapted from a public information map at the Mitsubishi Tunnel factory)

While the bomb and its effects were equally deadly to all humans in its path, urban geography and residence led its effects to be felt disproportionately by certain groups of people. A large proportion of Nagasaki's Christian community lived and then perished in the Urakami area, as did prisoners incarcerated at a site within the present-day Peace Park. Many Chinese labourers and even more people of Korean descent lived or worked in the area. The Urakami district was also a place of congregation for *burakamin* or outcaste peoples, and they too were victims. Neither should we neglect such local victims as those of the Shiroyama Elementary School, located 500 metres from the hypocentre; the blast killed 29 teachers and about 110 students. With the Medical College of Nagasaki University also proximate to the hypocentre, a total of 979 university teachers and students perished in the bombing: 897 from the Medical College (including Specialized School of Medicine and Specialized School of Pharmaceutics), 54 from Nagasaki Normal School,

Figure 2. Fat Man bomb Assembled at Tinian, 1 August 1945. (Source: US National Archives, courtesy Wikipedia Commons)

27 from Nagasaki Higher Commercial School and one from Nagasaki Youth Normal School.

Stepping back from the nuclear bombings, it is important to showcase the conventional area bombings of Japan, at least to offer context on rapidly shifting norms relating to civilian victims in modern warfare. As Mark Selden has pointed out in a number of essays, World War II was a landmark in the development and deployment of technologies of mass destruction associated with air power. In Japan, the US air war reached peak intensity with area bombing and climaxed with the atomic bombing of Japanese cities and Japan's 15 August 1945 surrender. The Mariana Islands had been captured in 1944, which placed Japanese cities within effective range of B-29 'Superfortress' bombers at a time when Japan's air and naval power was depleted, leaving them virtually defenceless. Incendiary raids became the new norm and removed the line between civilian and combatants that exercises in 'precision bombing' had attempted to blur. According to Japanese police statistics, the 65 raids on Tokyo between 6 December 1944 and 13 August 1945 resulted in 137,582 casualties, 787,145 homes and buildings destroyed, and 2,625,279 people displaced. Most of these missions were authorized by Curtis LeMay, who was appointed to lead the 21st Bomber Command in the Pacific in January 1945. Going on to serve as chief of staff of the US air force (1961–65), LeMay was widely reported as making such statements as: 'There are no innocent civilians,' and 'all war is immoral,' sentiments he would repeat with respect to the future US bombing of Korea and Vietnam. The full fury of firebombing and napalm was unleashed on the night of 9–10

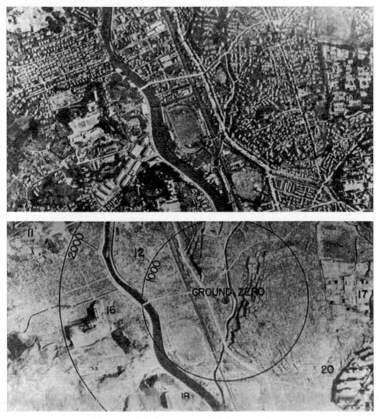

Figure 3. Nagasaki, Japan, before and after the atomic bombing of 9 August 1945. (Source: U.S. National Archives: RG 77-MDH, courtesy Wikipedia Commons)

March 1945 when LeMay sent 334 B-29s low over Tokyo from the Mariana Islands.

The figure of roughly 100,000 deaths, provided by Japanese and American authorities, may arguably be low. With an estimated 1.5 million people living in the burned-out areas, casualties may have been several times higher, more likely in the range of 200,000 than 100,000. All up some hundred Japanese cities and towns were destroyed.

Unlike the other target cities, Nagasaki had been conventionally bombed five times in the year prior to the atomic bombing and the residents were well drilled with respect to potential air raids. Although shipyards and dock areas in the southwest part of the city had been targeted, the first air raid of 11 August 1944 hit an urban area; the second of 2 April 1945 hit a dock area; the third of 29 July 1945 hit the Kawanami Shipyard; and the Mitsubishi Nagasaki Shipyard and railway yards were hit on 1 August 1945. Needless to say, all these raids incurred civilian casualties, including Allied POWs, in a situation where industrial and residential zoning was not clear. Neither had Nagasaki adopted the government policy of sending children to the countryside for protection – or labour – such as implemented in the last years of the war with respect to Tokyo and other large cities. The ordinary citizens of Nagasaki share one thing with their counterparts in Hiroshima: terrible as this conventional bombing may have been, they could not have had a premonition of the apocalyptic future to come.

The Atomic Bombings and the Surrender Debate

Next to the decision to drop the bombs, no other subject has agitated historians more than the quest to expose the logic behind Japan's belated surrender. In the Potsdam Declaration of 26 July 1945 (also later agreed by the Soviets), the Allies called for Japan's unconditional surrender, the alternative being 'prompt and utter destruction'. As is well documented, Japan sought to make its surrender conditional on the preservation of the imperial institution and this was specifically stated in correspondence between Foreign Minister Togo Shigenori on 21 July re a proposed mission by the Japanese politician Prince Konoye Fumimaro to Moscow 'to bring an end to the war with the good offices of the Soviet Government.' For weeks, Japan insisted upon the condition of preserving the emperor system 'even if the war drags on and it becomes clear that it will take much more bloodshed . . . so long as the enemy demands unconditional surrender' (From Moscow, Ambassador Sato Naotake had already advocated unconditional surrender provided the Imperial House was preserved, 20 July 1945). Tokyo had no idea that the Soviets had already committed to the Allies that it would declare war on Japan. Unknowing of this Soviet commitment, Tokyo fruitlessly pursued this diplomatic approach for several weeks.

Radical scholar Gar Alperovitz asserts the bomb was deployed against an already defeated Japan to deter Soviet expansionism. As such, he argues, the bombs were unnec-essary and that this was understood by policymakers at the time. In his 2004 book Paul Ham, the Australian correspon-dent of the *Sunday Times* of London, echoes the Alperovitz thesis that the bombings had little impact on the eventual outcome of the Pacific War, albeit adding some qualifications and elaborations. A greater threat than nuclear weapons in Tokyo's eyes in driving Japan to surrender, he declares, was fear of Russia and a communist takeover. Insofar as civilians as opposed to industrial sites were the main targets, the dropping of the atomic bombs was not primarily a strategic action – the civilian hearts of the two cities were targeted; not explicitly industrial complexes. As Ham spells out in an Epilogue, no sooner had Japan surrendered than the US commenced strategic nuclear planning against the Soviet Union, with Moscow responding by constructing its own nuclear arsenal. In other words, in unleashing weapons of mass destruction upon Hiroshima and Nagasaki, the military-industrial complex in the United States had taken on a life of its own around science and politics.

Others beg to differ (at least in detail). As analyzed by National Security Archive historians, US Army intercepts of Japanese diplomatic cable traffic from the end of July and early August show that the Japanese were far from ready to surrender. According to Herbert Bix, for months Emperor Hirohito had believed that the 'outlook for a negotiated peace could be improved if Japan fought and won one last decisive battle', thus Hirohito delayed surrender, continuing to 'procrastinate until the bomb was dropped and the Soviets attacked.'

The possibility of modifying the concept of unconditional surrender so that it guaranteed the continuation of the Emperor Showa reign remained hotly contested within the US government. Here senior State Department officials, Undersecretary Joseph Grew on one side and Assistant Secretary Dean Acheson and Archibald MacLeish on the other, engaged in vigorous debate. As Selden and Selden remark, there is cruel irony in the fact that only after the dropping of the bomb on Hiroshima and Nagasaki, the US softened its unconditional surrender provisions with respect to the Emperor. In the event, Hirohito continued to occupy the throne in the US vision of Japan as an 'imperial democracy'. From the Japanese perspective, procrastination over the surrender in order to ensure the survival of the Japanese royal house cost the nation at least a millions of its citizens, not only victims of the bomb but also those who died in Soviet prison camps in Manchuria or were otherwise blocked from returning.

The Bomb and Surrender as Viewed by *The Mainichi*

It is hard to believe that, given the firebombing of Tokyo, national newspapers still circulated, including even an English-language edition of *The Mainichi*. We are fortunate, as its reportage offers a unique optic upon then prevailing understandings (and misunderstandings) of the bombing from the Japanese side. As misleadingly reported in the 6 August edition, 'heavy damage' over Hiroshima was inflicted by a small number of B-29s dropping a new type of bomb by parachute. This of course was the uranium-type bomb dubbed by the Americans 'Little Boy'. Two days on, the full dimension of the disaster was still under-reported, just as it would take many hours for the reality to be grasped in army headquarters. On 8 August 1945, *The Mainichi*, as with other Japanese newspapers, dutifully published the Imperial War Rescript declaring war on the US and the British Empire. First promulgated on 8 December 1941, the War Rescript was reprinted on the 8th day of every month down until the surrender. It is all the more the ironic that this final reprinting appeared two days after US President Harry S. Truman's call for Japan's surrender, warning it to 'expect a rain of ruin from the air, the like of which has never been seen on this earth.' On 9 August the Americans dropped the plutonium-implosion type 'Fat Man' bomb over Nagasaki. Over the intervening days, as information seeped out of total devastation in Hiroshima, *The Mainichi* acknowledged the new type of bomb as 'atom'. Nevertheless, on 10 August it published a piece reporting the investigation of a military official who claimed that the bombs were survivable by taking shelter and wearing appropriate apparel! Also on 10 August *The Mainichi* reported – misleadingly – that Japanese forces were defending themselves against Soviet forces who had commenced their Manchuria offensive. Fateful days of indecision followed (both in Tokyo and Washington) and with US military planners weighing a number of scenarios, albeit with the prospect of an American landing on Kyushu receding amid the triumphalism in Washington that bombs had worked and with at least two other bombs readied in line with other (more terrible) scenarios.

The Emperor's recorded announcement of his Imperial Rescript, finally broadcast over the radio at noon on Wednesday 15 August, cleared the air but with the timing a matter of controversy down to this day. Dramatically (at least for English readers) on 16 August, *The Mainichi* published an English version of the (surrender) Rescript along with the banner headline, 'Greater East Asia War End: Imperial Rescript Granted: His Majesty Accepts 4-Power Proclamation to Spare Mankind From Terrors, Destruction of Atom Bomb'. On 17 August, *The Mainichi* offered a photograph of a fallen wireless transmitter (dropped simultaneously with the bombs) but still no panoramic shot (although later editions did indeed include such pictures). The failure of Foreign Minister Tojo Hideki to seek a negotiated peace with the Soviet Union was also noted, as was the abrogation of the Russo–Japanese neutrality treaty and the entry of the Soviet Union into the war. (In fact, Molotov had informed Tokyo of the abrogation of the pact on 5 August and the Soviets launched their Manchurian campaign four days later.) Both the bomb (or the second bomb) and/or the Soviet threat have featured regularly in speculations as to the timing of the capitulation, linked with diplomatic plays to ensure the preservation of the imperial line. On 2 September, Japanese representatives signed the instrument of surrender on board the USS *Missouri*, effectively ending World War II and this was solemnly recorded in *The Mainichi* of 3 September, along with the proclamation of the Emperor calling upon his subjects to abide by the terms of the surrender and to immediately suspend hostile actions.

Surveying the Devastated Landscape: The Fat Man Bomb over Nagasaki

Sweeney, who also commanded the instrument plane for the Hiroshima bomb mission, later visited Nagasaki accompanied by a party of 20 which included Brigadier General Paul Tibbets (the commander of the aircraft which dropped the bomb on Hiroshima). Their visit of early September is described in Sweeney's 1997 book *War's End*. As noted, US naval personnel were waiting on board vessels anchored in the harbour until scientific survey teams were sent in first to test for radioactivity. Tibbets also reports on this visit in an autobiography. Tibbets also gives a report on this same visit to Nagasaki. As he notes, after the signing of the peace treaty aboard the battleship *Missouri* in Tokyo harbour on 2 September, scientists from the Manhattan Project were anxious to get into Japan to check the results of their creations with respect to Hiroshima and Nagasaki:

> They wanted to find out the levels of radiation and determine how long it would linger. What was the most dangerous result of the new weapon: the explosive force, the intense heat, the radiation? We secured the approval of General MacArthur to accompany the occupying forces to Tokyo immediately, and from there to visit the bombed cities. In my security detachment were six Nisei who were born in Hawaii of Japanese parents. Because they spoke the Japanese language fluently, we took them along as interpreters.

As Tibbets recorded, the group was accompanied from Tokyo to Nagasaki via nearby Omura airport by Tsuzuki Masao, professor of radiology at Tokyo University medical school, then the leading Japanese authority on the biological effects of radiation. Also holding the rank of rear admiral in the Japanese Navy, Tsuzuki offers an example of the way that the American occupation forces put such 'enemy' figures to work. On 12 October 1945 MacArthur set up the Joint Commission for the Investigation of the Effects of the Atomic Bombs, also bringing Tsuzuki on board with a team of more than 90 Japanese physicians and scientists. Although a preliminary report was issued by the Joint Commission, much of the data was not released.

We should not be surprised. As Jordan establishes, a grey area exists in the history of the Hiroshima/Nagasaki bombings during the 1945–1947 period. The results of medical studies performed by the US army were not disclosed until long after the event. Even though there 'may have been' significant casualties in this period from fallout and radioactive contamination in these two cities, the US military-industrial complex, in full Cold War mode, already advocated the potential use of A-bombs as tactical weapons, 'and would definitely have wanted to suppress evidence of risks from fallout, in order to present them as "clean" weapons differing from conventional explosives only in their potency.'[1]

Australian Journalist Wilfred Burchett

Australian journalist Wilfred Burchett arrived in Hiroshima on 3 September 1945, duly filing a dispatch that appeared two days later in the London *Daily Express*. Touted as the first foreign journalist to witness and report on the bombing aftermath, his visit also overlapped with the arrival of an official American team of journalists. Nevertheless, Burchett's was the first eyewitness story on the atomic bombings to be prominently headlined in a Western newspaper, a veritable scoop.

As Burchett explains in *Shadows of Hiroshima*, having arrived in Tokyo Bay on 28 August with the US Navy, accompanied by some 500 other journalists seeking to cover the Japanese surrender ceremony on board the *Missouri*, he detached

---

1   Bertrand A. Jordan, 'The Hiroshima/Nagasaki Survivor Studies,' 1512.

himself from the group by making the short journey to central Tokyo station and struck out alone. Making contact in central Tokyo with the Japanese Domei News Agency, he departed for Hiroshima by train, arriving just one month after the bomb had dropped. In so doing Burchett acted in defiance of General MacArthur's orders to the journalists to keep away from the A-bombed cities. Vital in the event, his Domei contact in Hiroshima facilitated his famous dispatch, which was tapped out by Morse code, duly received in Tokyo, couriered to Yokohama and, clearing censorship after some dispute and revision, relayed on to London.

Appearing on the front page of the London *Daily Express* 5 September 1945 edition, Burchett's story bore the dramatic headlines,

THE ATOMIC PLAGUE
'I Write This as a Warning to the World'
DOCTORS FALL AS THEY WORK

Though little understood at the time, Burchett served early warning as to the effects of atomic radiation. He also correctly labelled the bombing as an atomic 'testing ground'. As he observed, and as he learned from the Japanese scientists and doctors he encountered, people who survived and should have recovered succumbed to a little-understood illness or the other effects of atomic radiation. Burchett also first put this experience into book form as a postscript to his *Democracy with a Tommygun*. Walking through the streets of Hiroshima, as Burchett wrote, 'one had the feeling of having been transplanted into some death stricken other planet . . .

Figure 4. Front page of the *Daily Express*, 5 September 1945, by Wilfred Burchett.

There was nothing but awful devastation and desolation . . . mists seemed to issue forth from fissures in the soil. There was a dark, acrid sulphurous smell . . . .'

Although still awed by American technology and still holding to the view that the firebombing of Japanese cities was necessary, his Hiroshima experience also led to a profound transformation of attitude. Burchett issued his own call for peace in 1946. With prescience, he understood that any country reasonably advanced in scientific research (such as Britain) could produce a bomb and of far greater power than Hiroshima. Burchett then probably didn't realize then that wartime Japan also hosted a nuclear program, possibly with Axis cooperation that might have included the construction of cyclotrons which could be used to separate fissionable material from ordinary uranium, though far from producing a bomb. Prudently, as Burchett advised (and the message conveyed by the cities of

Nagasaki and Hiroshima unto today), 'international control is the only way of avoiding world catastrophe. Control or catastrophe are the only two alternatives, and control cannot be effective without a strong world organization.' How right he was and, as mentioned below, he would be a welcome visitor in Hiroshima over the years.

US Journalist George Weller

Veteran American World War II *Chicago Daily News* reporter George Weller (1907–2002) was the first independent outsider to reach Nagasaki. This was on 6 September 1945, exactly four weeks after the atomic bombing (and three days after Burchett's arrival in Hiroshima). As with Burchett, Weller had defied orders of General MacArthur forbidding reporters from entering either of the nuclear-bombed cities. Arriving by boat and train and passing himself off to the Japanese as an American military official, his dispatches never reached his editors at the *Chicago Daily Times* or even made it past MacArthur's censors. Unable to sell his story to an American publisher, the *Mainichi Shimbun* did oblige. Believed lost, a carbon copy of his original writings only surfaced 60 years later and was published by his son Anthony in 2006. Weller may not have preceded American officials anxious to collect data on their most recent test but, as mentioned below, he was ten days ahead of a Soviet team that had similar goals in mind.

Having spent a total of three weeks in Nagasaki including the nearby Allied POW camps, some of which he 'opened', Weller went on to produce a manuscript totalling about 80,000 words in unedited form. Son Anthony explains that all his father's dispatches were 'expanded' from a ready-for-telegram language that reporters of the day were accustomed to using. Due to the costs of sending stories back home, this compressed 'cablese' removed all obvious words. One such dispatch, as typed in its original version and written at 1 a.m on the morning of 9 September, reads:

> The atomic bomb's peculiar "disease", uncured because it is untreated and untreated because it is undiagnosed, is still snatching away lives here. Men, women and children with no outward marks of injury are dying daily in hospitals, some after having walked around for three or four weeks thinking they have escaped. The doctors here have every modern medicament, but candidly confessed in talking to the writer – the first Allied observer to reach Nagasaki since the surrender – that the answer to the malady is beyond them. Their patients, though their skins are whole, are simply passing away under their eyes.

Truman issued a confidential memorandum demanding silence about the bomb from all US media, and it is clear that Weller's dispatches fell under this censorship regime. Nevertheless, Weller always maintained that since MacArthur was determined to be known as the vanquisher of Japan (despite denials of presidential ambition), he did not want to promote the bombs' success at the cost of his own. Likewise, he reasoned, a candid report on the radiation suffering in the Nagasaki hospitals under his control not only contradicted US government assurances but also, more importantly, could only embarrass MacArthur before the American people.

Another detail that came to light was that even a month after the bomb, MacArthur as Supreme Commander had failed to provide medical assistance to the devastated (and such aid would only arrive six weeks later courtesy of the Navy). According to son Anthony, as Weller visited all the hospital facilities that still existed in the ruins of the city, he was struck immediately by the absence of any American medical personnel there – four weeks later, there were still no doctors or nurses – and also by the great precision and care with which the Japanese doctors had already cata-logued the effects of the bomb on individual organs of the body. . . . And over the next few days, he was as astonished as the Japanese doctors by what he referred to in his reports as 'Disease X'.

Years later, Weller sought out a meeting with Burchett in Paris. They failed to meet but, as Weller reportedly told Burchett over the telephone, 'I covered the *Missouri* surrender ceremony and then set out to do what you did.' Describing his ruse and journey:

> 'We got to Nagasaki and to those hospitals which were still functioning, piecing together a complete analysis. The medical personnel were completely cooperative. I wrote a series of articles totalling 25,000 words. As a loyal disciplined member of the press corps, I sent the material to MacArthur's press headquarters for clearance and transmission.'

As Burchett found out after continuing on to Guam, 'MacArthur had "killed" the lot. I had always been an enemy of MacArthur's censorship. Now I think he decided to punish me.'[2]

Nevertheless, it was thus left to popular writer John Hersey who first introduced Americans to atomic bomb survivors in a celebrated long essay in 1946 for *The New Yorker* (issued in book form as *Hiroshima*). As Hersey weaved the lives of six Japanese into the narrative, he put a human face on the bomb's victims and graphically depicted their suffering. Initially banned in Japan, a Japanese translation of *Hiroshima* was first published in 1949. From the beginning, however, there were critics. Many of the early critics even declared that Japan was trying to surrender when blindsided by the nuclear weapon. While hugely influential and aptly hailed as a landmark in journalism, not all in the US would then or now so readily accept a victim's perspective.

As Mark Selden has written in a reflective essay on the conventional and nuclear bombings of Japan,

> The US would celebrate the power of the bomb in powerful visual statements of the birth of the nuclear era that would be directed at the entire world on 6 August, on 9 August and in the decades that followed.

As he explains, close-up images of victims of American bombing captured on film by Japanese photographers in now-iconic photographs of Hiroshima, Nagasaki and Tokyo had been banned. The US occupation authorities maintained a monopoly on scientific and medical information about the

---

2   As reprinted in *Shadows of Hiroshima*, 44–45.

effects of the atomic bomb through the work of the Atomic Bomb Casualty Commission, which treated the data gathered in studies of *hibakusha* as privileged information rather than making the results available for the treatment of victims or providing financial or medical support to aid victims. The US also stood by its official denial of the ravages associated with radiation.

As John Dower explains, censorship by US occupation forces, lasting from August 1946 to April 1952 resulted in a 'remarkable occurrence', namely that 'the public had virtually no access to graphic images of Hiroshima and Nagasaki until seven years after the bombs were dropped.' As he points out, the first full set of atom bomb photos was published in the August 1952 edition of *Asahi Gurafu* magazine, followed in the same year with Yamahata Yosuke's photo record of the destruction in Nagasaki, as discussed below. As Dower further comments, even though Japanese filmmakers had produced several hours of black-and-white footage of the nuclear destruction in the early weeks following the bombing, the films were confiscated by the US government and remained censored until the mid-1960s. Only after being declassified were the most dramatic frames privately edited into a short documentary titled *Hiroshima Nagasaki, 1945*. In 1952, the Japanese docufiction film *Genbaku no Ko* (Children of Hiroshima) was produced by the acclaimed director Shindo Kaneto, at the invitation of the decidedly leftist Japan Teacher's Union. Entered in the 1953 Cannes film festival, it gained a wide audience globally.

Japanese Military Photographer Yamahata Yosuke

From 1940, the Singapore-born Yamahata Yosuke (1917–66) worked as a military photographer in China and elsewhere in Asia before returning to Japan in 1942. On 10 August 1945, a day after the Nagasaki bombing and still in military employ, Yamahata began to photograph the devastation. Over a period of about 12 hours he took around a hundred exposures; by late afternoon he had taken his final photographs, near a first aid station north of the city. In a single day, he had completed the only extensive photographic record of the immediate aftermath of the atomic bombing of either Hiroshima or Nagasaki. His photographs gained quick publication in the 21 August issue of *Mainichi Shimbun*.[3] Even so, with the original images confiscated by the American military under strict censorship rules, the full set only re-emerged 50 years later, in 1995.

NEVERTHELESS, THE IMAGES trickled out. After SCAP's restrictions on coverage of the effects of the atomic bomb were lifted in 1952, Yamahata's photographs of Nagasaki appeared in the 29 September issue of *Life*. The same year, they appeared in the book *Kiroku-shashin: Genbaku no Nagasaki*. Some also appeared in the exhibition and book *The Family of Man*. Subsequently, 24 Yamahata images of the city in ruins appeared in the *Mainichi Shimbun* selected from a larger collection compiled by a former American military policeman.

---

3   For a profile on Yamahata, see Ayelet Zohar in David P. Chandler, Robert Cribb and Li Narangoa, eds., *End of Empire: 100 Days in 1945 that changed Asia and the World* (Copenhagen: NIAS Press, 2016), 41–42.

Figure 5. Yamahata Yosuke: portrait of the photographer at the bomb site. (Source: Yamahata Yosuke, copyright: Yamahata Shogo)

Having arrived in Nagasaki, Yamahata described it as 'hell on Earth'. Those who had just barely survived the intense radiation-their eyes burned and their exposed skin scalded-wandered around aimlessly with only sticks to lean on, waiting for relief. 'Not a single cloud blocked the direct rays of the August sunlight, which shone down mercilessly

Figure 6. Nagasaki in the morning of 10 August 1945. Takara-machi, 1.6 km south of the blast hypocentre. (Source: Yamahata Yosuke, copyright: Yamahata Shogo)

Figure 7. Cremating the dead and coping with the disaster, Nagasaki, 10 August 1945. (Source: Yamahata Yosuke, copyright: Yamahata Shogo)

on Nagasaki, on that second day after the blast.' As quoted by *The Independent* in 1952, he wrote:

> Human memory has a tendency to slip, and critical judgment to fade, with the years and with changes in life-style and circumstance. But the camera, just as it seized the grim realities of that time, brings the stark facts of seven years ago before our eyes without the need for the slightest embellishment.

The Saving a Million American Lives Narrative

The key American narrative – or myth actually – surrounding the atomic bombings and one that remains resilient over the years is that a million American lives were saved, as that would be the certain cost in the event of a land invasion. Needless to say, such a view begs many questions about Japanese surrender scenarios, namely that no invasion of Japan prior to November was even contemplated, that the surrender of Japan was already imminent in July; that the Soviet entry into the war on 9 August was a major factor in the Japanese surrender; and therefore that the atomic bombs probably saved no American lives at all. It also ignores the hubris of Truman and his truly hawkish advisors surrounding the production of the bomb itself. Finally, this view seems to ignore the de facto defeat of Japan, with its war industries practically demolished, its battleships and aircraft neutralized and its population half starved to death by the American naval blockade.

Nonetheless, the million-lives-saved view appears to be shared by the surviving Allied POWs who gained their liberty in the wake of the bombing and the surrender or, in some cases, even before the surrender. Advocates for (and/or apologists for) using the bomb can with justification point to the total war mindset of Japanese militarists who were prepared to sacrifice the nation and its population to protect the Emperor's honour. Further, more than a few believed collective punishment was appropriate. After all, Pearl Harbor, Japanese war crimes, treatment of POWS and Pacific war battles including sacrifices of Okinawans and Americans alike were then very recent memory. Obviously the American narrative jars with the Japan-as-victim narrative, which enjoys as much acceptance across Japan as the American narrative has in the US; the American narrative hasn't the slightest acceptance in the atom-bombed cities.

In 1994 the Smithsonian Institution's National Air and Space Museum was beginning to mount an exhibit titled 'The Crossroads: The End of World War II, the Atomic Bomb and the Cold War'. The central artefact of the exhibit, set to open on the 50th anniversary of the atomic bombing of Hiroshima and Nagasaki, was the cockpit and nose section of the *Enola Gay*. Although well-crafted and offering different perspectives, including controversies about the atomic bombings, the exhibition was torpedoed by conservative opinion along with many US World War II veterans who proclaimed that they owed their lives to the atomic bombs. On 23 September 1994, the US Senate passed a resolution, by a vote of 99 to 1, declaring: 'the role of the Enola Gay during World War II was momentous in helping to bring World War II to a merciful end, which resulted in saving the lives of Americans and Japanese'. With the Senate resolution reviling the

Museum's exhibit as 'revisionist and offensive to many World War II veterans,' what many people viewed as a truth – that the bomb had saved hundreds of thousands of American soldiers who otherwise would have died in the invasion of Japan – was transformed into a self-serving myth.

Reflecting upon the popular American view, H. Bruce Franklin wrote in the *LA Review of Books* in 2014 that

> [t]he gulf between public belief and the prodigious research and analysis by historians remains wide, although as disapproval of nuclear weapons has increased among younger Americans that gap has narrowed.

Even as polls indicate that the post-war taboo against the first use of nuclear weapons holds strong among the US public, still another strand of research challenges their implications. For example, Sagan and Valentino conducted a poll with reference to contemporary Iran. Respondents when placed in the mindset of making trade-offs between bombing non-combatants and saving American lives, tended to replicate Truman's fateful decision of 1945. This is a theme to which we return, in the context of a discussion of the 2017–18 North Korean missile crisis.

Authors Paul Ham and Craig Collie

Did the means – 180,000 total dead and wounded on the days that the bombs were dropped and later tens of thousands more as a result of radiation poisoning – justify the end of bringing the Second World War to a close? Was it necessary, indeed, to drop the bombs at all? These questions are at the heart of both Paul Ham's *Hiroshima Nagasaki* and Craig Collie's *Nagasaki*, a dramatic presentation of real-time events in Tokyo, Moscow and even inside the *Bockscar* cockpit, set against the backdrop of everyday life in Nagasaki. For them, the notion that the bomb forced Japan to surrender unconditionally was a position bound to strike a resonance with many readers, although not one necessarily accepted by the victims. Ham recounts a familiar story of deadlock between Japanese diplomats who knew the war was lost and military leaders who asserted that national suicide was preferable to surrender. He believes that, given the Soviet declaration of war against Japan on 8 August (in his mind, more important than the bombs in ending the war) and the continuing US naval blockade, an American invasion would not have been necessary; but he admits that at the least the atomic bombings of Hiroshima and Nagasaki gave an irresolute Emperor and his military chiefs an excuse to end the war. 'Tokyo was able to surrender without conceding defeat on the battlefield, where it mattered most to the samurai mind.' 'Tokyo did not surrender to protect the Japanese people from the weapon; the leadership had shown not the slightest duty of care towards these "innocent lives"', he writes. Rather, Japan cited the bombings as only a face-saving device that enabled Hirohito and his generals to claim they were ending the war as martyrs. In fact, they were trying to save their own skins.

Chapter 3

Origins of the Nagasaki Peace Discourse

By the early 1950s, the full horrors of a post-nuclear world had sunk into the global general public. Around the world, citizens began to make their views known, at least where that was possible. The 1950s also coincided with a period when the US and Great Britain, followed by France in 1960, not to mention the USSR in 1949 followed by China in 1964, began testing nuclear weapons. As discussed in Chapter 4, during the period when the US tested nuclear weapons in the Pacific, peace movements emerged in Japan and, in 1954, converged to form a unified 'Japanese Council Against Atomic and Hydrogen Bombs'. Almost simultaneously the Soviet Union and its satellites sought to capture peace movements, and Nagasaki weighed into this calculation (as symbolized in Nagasaki's Peace Park today). But the US controlled the nuclear narrative in Japan, at least until SCAP wound down in 1952. As this chapter reveals, in the early post-war period considerable tensions emerged between local A-bomb sufferers in Nagasaki, American occupiers, City Hall and the national government as to their suffering and victim-hood. It was in this environment of early post-war political reform and economic reconstruction that the Nagasaki Peace Discourse emerged with its particular pacifist message, at least when compared with the more strident victim activist message for which Hiroshima was already known.

As Chad Diehl interprets, whereas Hiroshima quickly moved to memorialize the suffering and destruction caused by the bomb, Nagasaki sought to put the war behind them. Encouraged by local politicians and American occupation personnel, Nagasaki adopted a vision of an 'international cultural city' around the slogan, 'Peace starts at Nagasaki'. While this apparent sense of resignation might be attributed to Catholic piety, still not all among the Catholic community much less the mass of non-Catholic atomic bomb sufferers joined this consensus. By the late 1950s, contestation among the stakeholders had begun. By the 1970s, the 'peace movement' had become not only politicized but also highly factionalized.

The Nagai Takeshi Narrative

Perhaps no other name associated with the atomic bombing of Nagasaki has received as much attention – whether as sufferer, anti-nuclear war publicist, or voice of Catholic victims – as Nagai Takeshi. Born in Matsue in distant Shimane Prefecture and trained as a physician specializing in radiation, he accepted a position at the Nagasaki Medical College in 1928. Nagai had earlier served as a doctor attached to an Imperial Japanese army unit in Manchuria, and as such he was already a participant in Japan's wider war, indeed was understood to be in Nanjing at the time of the massacre. He converted to Christianity in 1934 and took his place among the Christian community in Urakami. At the moment of the atomic bombing, Nagai was in his office at the Medical College, only 700 metres from the hypocentre. With his wife killed by the bomb and house destroyed, he immediately joined other surviving Japanese medical staff in treating the victims. He also penned a 100-page medical report based upon observations and, until his death from leukaemia on 1 May 1951, offered scientific and philosophical elaborations.

Besides achieving best-seller status in Japan, with his books translated into numerous languages, Nagai also reached an international audience. His *We of Nagasaki* was the first book on the subject, published in London by left-wing internationalist publisher Victor Gollancz in 1951. This work served as my first book-length introduction to the subject. I purchased a copy from a second-hand bookstore in Melbourne, Australia, just prior to my own departure for Nagasaki. A library endorsement reveals that this copy was originally owned by a local Catholic library. Going by the frequency of borrowings in 1953 as revealed by still legible date stamps, this had been a popular book, perhaps meeting the interest of an extremely curious Western audience. Similarly, *The Bells of Nagasaki* (Nagasaki no Kane), first appearing in Japanese in 1949, gained even more publicity inside Japan with the release of a movie of the same name in September 1950. Nevertheless, even this work with its obviously Christian symbolism was subject to GHQ censorship, including the addition of an appendix on Japanese atrocities in the Philippines. Translations into other languages soon followed.

While Nagai's works have been interpreted as exemplars of Christian piety, his fatalistic interpretation of the bombing of Nagasaki as 'providence of God' and the victims as 'sacrificial lambs' has been subject to much comment (by *hibakusha*) and even interrogation (by media and intellectuals). As

Miyamoto Yuki interprets, while Nagai's understanding of suffering may be in line with Catholic dogma and, indeed, position which may have eased reconciliation between ose who dropped the bomb and those who suffered, it may also have helped to shift responsibility away from 'Japan as aggressor'. As Diehl points out, published from 1948 with America's blessing and even on paper supplied by SCAP, Nagai's books preached anti-communism to hundreds of thousands of readers while portraying the Cold War as a struggle between Christian values and communism. By endorsing Nagai's books, American occupation officials show they understood the consonance between Nagai's views on the atomic bombing and the American narrative of Japan as aggressor. American censors fine-tuned this narrative, for example by insisting he focus upon the Pacific War as opposed to the much longer time-frame of the invasion of China, and that he delete mention of the original civilian target of the bombing as opposed to the military. By adding the chapter appendix on Japanese atrocities in Christian Manila, Diehl argues, the Americans could equate one atrocity with another. SCAP's censorship authority ended in 1952 and the Manila appendix was removed from post-1952 editions of *Bells of Nagasaki*. The shift in popular Japanese mindset from wartime victimizer to post-war victim was already underway.

In recent times, Nagai has been honoured by the Catholic Church with the title of 'servant of God', taken to be the first step towards Roman Catholic sainthood. The site on Santos Dori (one of the few streets in Nagasaki memorializing the Portuguese Catholic era) where his reconstructed house is appropriately museumed and serves virtually as a pilgrimage site. Moreover, a corner of the Atomic Bomb Museum itself is dedicated to Nagai and displays various of his writings and publications. He was, in fact, a *hibakusha*, even though he died before the term had entered popular parlance.[1]

Enter the *Hibakusha*

Atomic bomb victims in Japan were of course recognized as such by the local medical establishment and, indeed, Nagasaki boasts a Nagasaki Atomic Radiation Hospital. Nevertheless, official recognition of victims as *hibakusha* remained for the future, especially with respect to the complex rules that came to surround both definition and eligibility for compensation. Indeed, the initial public response to atomic bomb survivors and their children, however irrational, was stigmatization, especially when it came to prospects of marriage. The comparison might be made with Fukushima victims or nuclear refugees who likewise face discrimination today.

---

1   Still, the Catholic church is alert. Notably, in January 2018 Pope Francis endorsed an iconic photo of a Nagasaki boy carrying his dead brother, taken by US Marine photographer Joe O'Donnell shortly after the Nagasaki bombing. In April, the Pope expressed strong interest in visiting Nagasaki and Hiroshima. In July, during a meeting of the Catholic Bishops' Conference of Japan, the Archbishop of Nagasaki diocese, Mitsuaki Takami, a second-generation *hibakusha* himself, interpreted that '(the Pope) was likely intuitively convinced that this will serve as a message to the current situation, in which the Treaty on the Prohibition of Nuclear Weapons is not endorsed by nuclear weapon states and the countries under their umbrellas, and nuclear arms are proliferating beyond control.' Kentaro Yamano, 'Japan Catholics to get photo of Nagasaki boy signed by pope' (*The Asahi Shimbun*, 25 July 2018).

By the 1950s and with civil society support, *hibakusha* and their descendants became increasingly vocal in demanding government compensation and in promoting the anti-nuclear message. An important landmark for Nagasaki atomic bomb sufferers was the establishment in June 1956 of what would become the city's largest organization in support of *hibakusha*, namely the Nagasaki Atom Bomb Survivors Council (Hisaikkyo). As Susan Southard relates, Hisaikkyo not only campaigned for the abolition of nuclear weapons, but also sought recognition from the government of their medical condition as well as compensation. One of the founders, Taniguchi Sumiteru, went on to become a chairperson of the Japan Confederation of A- and H-Bomb Sufferers Organizations (Nihon Hidankyo). Also known for the scarlet-coloured burns to his back as depicted in an iconic photograph taken in January 1946, he went on to give a speech in May 2010 at the UN conference in New York on reviewing the Nuclear Non-Proliferation Treaty. He died in August 2017 at the age of 88.[2]

Nevertheless, severe challenges awaited the sufferers, especially as eligibility criteria seemed to be cumbersome and opaque by design. The Atomic Bomb Survivors Relief Law, enacted in 1995 and relating to both the Hiroshima and Nagasaki bombings without distinction, defines *hibakusha* as including people who were: within a few kilometres of the hypocentres of the bombs at the time of the dropping; within two kilometres of the hypocentres within two weeks of the bombings; exposed to radiation from fallout; or not yet born

---

2   Kyodo, 'Nagasaki A-bomb survivor and victims' advocate Taniguchi dies at 88,' *The Japan Times*, 30 August 2017.

but carried by pregnant women in any of these categories. As discussed in Chapter 6, it would not be until September 2015, some 20 years after the Supreme Court ruled in favour of Korean plaintiffs, that survivors who lived abroad would actually receive their pensions.[3] Updated annually on the anniversaries of the bombings, memorials record the names of all *hibakusha* known to have died since the bombings.

In Hiroshima (perhaps even more so than in Nagasaki), August becomes an occasion for intensified reflection on atomic bombs and agitation for nuclear disarmament – a tradition that dates back to the mid-1950s. The Hiroshima Peace Memorial Museum opened its doors in 1955 and the first Japanese anti-nuclear organizations emerged around the same time, initially on the political left. But whereas Hiroshima led, Nagasaki lagged. Sometimes this is expressed in Japanese as '*Ikari no Hiroshima, inori no Nagasaki*' (wrathful Hiroshima prayerful Nagasaki). As Miyamoto explains, this description echoes a pervasive if stereotypical perception held in Japan that the citizens of Hiroshima are more inclined to political action versus the 'religious' and peaceful responses of Nagasaki.

Still, *hibakusha* is a somewhat contested category, especially if we distinguish between those granted official *Hibakusha* status (with a capital H),); that is those coming under the Atomic Bomb Survivors Relief Law, and those who fail to meet the strict definitional criteria and are thus denied official recognition, even though they believe themselves to be members of the *hibakusha* community. While some *Hibakusha*

---

3   Editorial, 'Justice for A-bomb victims overseas,' *The Japan Times*, 22 September 2015.

have become feted individuals to be paraded at ceremonies and official visits, there are also angry *hibakusha* and/or supporters who rally against national government policies, and would-be *hibakusha* as with many Koreans who have still been denied status and pensions. Also, as alluded, there are those who fear discrimination and have even disguised their *hibakusha* backgrounds.[4] The march of time has of course levelled the playing field as *hibakusha* of all persuasions pass away. Perversely, however, the Fukushima nuclear disaster may have generated new (unofficial) *hibakusha*, whose membership includes those suffering thyroid disease and other radiation-linked nuclear medical complaints, just as worldwide victims of radiation poisoning might claim (or be claimed) to have something akin to *hibakusha* status. As discussed in Chapter 6, this is recognized at the Peace Park as with the positioning of an Australian monument to native Australian victims of British atomic testing.

---

4   Tetsuo Shintomi, 'Nagasaki hibakusha recalls struggle to dodge discrimination,' *The Japan Times*, 16 March 2015.

Chapter 4

The POW Experience: Contrary Narratives

Alongside other victims and 'stakeholders' when it comes to compensation and memorialization, we cannot neglect the Allied POWs including, in some accounts, the 350 who died instantly at the bomb's hypocentre along with survivors, many of whom were *hibakusha* in their own right (although few would survive to receive *Hibakusha* status). By 1944, hundreds of British, Dutch-Indonesian, Australian and American prisoners-of-war (POWs) worked as slave labourers in Mitsubishi's massive shipbuilding complex in Nagasaki. This was in addition to over 10,000 POWs interned across Kyushu in a veritable gulag of camps prefixed by 'Fukuoka' and answering to that command. In Nagasaki, Mitsubishi's workforce also included thousands of Korean labourers taken by force from their homeland, who worked under armed guard at the shipyard, in its many factories around the city, and in the company's two coal mines on islands just off the coast. On Hashima Island alone, at least 50 of the between 500 and 800 Koreans who worked in undersea mines between 1943 and 1945 were confirmed dead from accidents and violence. At the Mitsubishi-run Sakito Island coal mine, records reveal that 212 Koreans died. In August 1945 Korean miners were brought to Nagasaki to assist in the relief effort where like the others they were exposed to radiation.[1]

---

1 Documentation from Oka Masaharu Nagasaki Peace Museum.

In July 2015, several of these Nagasaki sites, including the shipyard (still operating) and the coal mines (closed decades ago), were approved by UNESCO for World Heritage listing as part of Japan's early industrialization. Given concerns in Korea that this memory was not well served, the listing of the shipyard and mines required extensive negotiations as to how the labourers should be described; the Tokyo government sought to avoid the term 'forced labour'. While Mitsubishi Heavy Industries has publicly apologized for its use of POW labour at its many mine sites, it has yet to apologize to those POWs forced to work at other sites, including the Nagasaki shipbuilding complex and has remained silent as to the way so many Koreans and Chinese came to work for them.[2] A legal challenge mounted against Mitsubishi by Korean forced labourers continues to languish, with the company asserting that the plaintiff's claims lapsed with the Korea–Japan Agreement on Reparations of 1965.[3] More generally, Japan has remained silent as to the way so many Koreans and Chinese came to work for them.

In the period leading up to the atomic bombing, 884 Allied POWs in the Nagasaki city region were divided between two main POW camps. The first was Koyagi Branch Camp (Fukuoka 2-B) on Koyagi Island in Nagasaki Harbour, where the number of POWs peaked at about 1,500. The second was the Nagasaki Mitsubishi Dockyard Branch Camp (Fukuoka 14-B) located in Saiwamachi (Urakami

2   Mich Broderick and David Palmer, 'Australian, British, Dutch and U.S. POWs: Living under the shadow of the Nagasaki Bomb,' *The Asia-Pacific Journal | Japan Focus* (Vol. 13, Issue 32, No. 4, 10 August 2015).

3   Documentation from Oka Masaharu Nagasaki Peace Museum.

District), established on 22 April 1943 and with different groups of POWs continuing to arrive through June 1944. The Fukuoka 14-B held 195 POWs (152 Dutch, 24 Australian and 19 British). Members of this camp included survivors of the *Tamabuko Maru*, which had been carrying 773 POWs from Singapore to Japan when it was sunk by an American submarine within sight of the Nagasaki coast on 24 June 1944, with 560 lives lost. The survivors were used by Mitsubishi Heavy Industry Company. Altogether seven of the Fukuoka 14-B camp POWs became direct victims of the atomic bombing, namely a work party of seven Dutch, while 113 other POWs had earlier died of overwork, accident, illness and malnutrition.

Another group of POWS were held at the Koyagi Branch Camp (Fukuoka 2-B), pending its establishment in October 1942 as the Nagasaki Branch of the Yahata Provisional POW Camp at Koyagi-mura, Nishisonogi-gun. In January 1943, it was reorganized as the Nagasaki Branch of the Fukuoka POW Camp and renamed Fukuoka No. 2 Branch Camp in the following month. These POWs were used by Kawanami Ship Building Company. Up until the end of the war, a total of 497 POWs (324 Dutch, 160 British, five American and eight with other nationalities) were imprisoned here.

A third group of POWs, albeit outside of the atom-bombed zone, was held at the Emukae Branch Camp (Fukuoka 24-B). Established in January 1945 as the Fukuoka No. 24 Branch Camp at Senryu Coal Mine, the POWs were used by Sumitomo Mining Company. Up until the end of the war, 267 POWs (117 British, 114 Australian, 35 American and one Dutch) were imprisoned here. Twenty died during imprisonment.[4]

Australian Alan Chick and his battalion had been captured by the Japanese on Timor Island prior to dispatch to Japan on the *Tamabuko Maru*. Together with other survivors of the US torpedo attack, he was rescued by a Japanese fishing boat off the Kyushu coast and delivered up to Nagasaki, where he was installed in the Fukuoka POW Camp 14 and put to work at the Mitsubishi steel foundry. Sited less than two kilometres from the atomic bomb hypocentre, he was knocked unconscious by the blast, awakening to a world of complete darkness. When the smoke cleared he saw destruction, fires and death everywhere. He had somehow survived, again.[5]

Following the US military takeover of the facility on 13 September 1945, it was transformed into a processing hub for Allied POWs arriving in Nagasaki from different parts of Kyushu. In only a few days, more than 10,000 were evacuated by ship to the Philippines where they received medical treatment and recuperated. The apocalyptic scenes of atom-bombed Nagasaki must have been a searing sight to the liberated POWs arriving from outside Nagasaki. Contrariwise, the sight of thousands of bedraggled and skeletal non-Japanese shuffling through the irradiated streets of Nagasaki prior to boarding their evacuation ships must have presented an incredible spectacle to local survivors.

---

4   Toru Fukubayashi, 'POW Camps in Japan Proper POW Research Network Japan.'

5   Broderick and Palmer, 'Australian, British, Dutch and U.S. POWs.'

There were Allied prisoners of other nationalities as well, including native subjects of the Dutch. An exhibition of never-before-seen US military photos hosted in the Atomic Bomb Museum in July 2018 reveals the arrival of the POWs in Nagasaki including a contingent of 'Indonesians'.[6] As Australian journalist Denis Warner wrote, 'Just how fortunate the Australians were became apparent from the fate of the Chinese . . . . Their billets were deep in corpses' (although some were seen escaping alive). What is surprising, and a fact Warner speculates about, is that the Australian group survived the bomb and even went on to outlive countrymen who were spared the bomb (and none of their deaths could be directly attributed to radiation). A number of the Australians returned to Nagasaki after the war, as with Peter McGrath-Kerr, the only member to have suffered radiation burns and who served as a guest of honour on the occasion of the 35th anniversary in 1980. Nevertheless, the message is rather ambiguous here, namely as to survivability of atomic radiation victims versus the long-term effects of radiation poisoning.

In *A Doctor's Sword,* author Bob Johnson traces Irish POW and Nagasaki atomic bomb survivor Aidan MacCarthy's journey. Born in 1913, MacCarthy had graduated with a medical degree from University College Cork before traveling to London, where he enlisted in the Royal Air Force. Captured in the fall of Singapore, as with Chick, he

6   Australian archives sources are more specific. National Archives of Australia (NAA) B3856, 140/11/3394 Prisoners of War recovered from Nagasaki, Japan – Includes a Nominal Roll, dated October 1945. Besides the ABCD group, they included Norwegians, South Africans, Czech, Portuguese, West Indians, 'Malays' and 'Arabs,' and with 127 unaccounted for at the time of evacuation.

was interned as a POW aboard a ship en route from Java to Japan when torpedoed by an American submarine. He was thus one of 38 people out of 780 prisoners to survive the sinking of the ship. But even that experience paled when, working as a POW in the Mitsubishi Steel & Arms Works in Nagasaki, he took shelter in a shed on the fateful day of the bombing. According to MacCarthy's biographer, he was the first non-Japanese doctor to assist civilians in the devastating aftermath of the atomic bomb. The title of the book (and a subsequent film) relates to the samurai sword given to MacCarthy by the Japanese POW camp commandant, 2nd Lieutenant Kusano Isao, after the Irishman shielded him from vengeful POWs following Japan's 15th August surrender. Another 'British' survivor account is that of Alistair Urquhart, author of *The Forgotten Highlander*. Living into his nineties, he became the last surviving member of the Scottish regiment the Gordon Highlanders.

A Dutch prisoner of war from Fukuoka Camp 14 (the Kawaminami shipyard), Dr Johannes Stellingwerff, went on to author a book titled (in translation from Dutch), *Fat Man in Nagasaki, Dutch POWs Killed by the Atomic Bomb*. Inter alia, he noted that the first American journalist to visit the city (a likely reference to Weller) did so on 9 September. Still others (US officials?) arrived, accompanying men in protective clothing who measured radioactivity. He further reported that, on 3 September 1945, three Swiss and one Swedish Red Cross representative arrived in Nagasaki to visit the ex-POWs. His book offers many captioned monochrome illustrations including those clandestinely drawn by Dutch POWs, images of the Fat Man bomb, a full-page sketch-map of the camp, and a detailed name-list of the Dutch POWs who perished in the camp. He also supplies details on the conditions of the Dutch POWs, including those involved in forced labour in nearby mines and Nagasaki Mitsubishi Dockyard. Additionally, he offers extensive eyewitness observations and recollections of surviving POWs on the dropping and effects of the Fat Man bomb. As explained, the Fukuoka camp was located approximately 800 metres from the epicentre. Fortunately, many POWs were working in more distant locations at the moment Fat Man exploded.

Dolf Winkler and Rene Schäfer also were Dutch POWs in Japan, both going on to author books and both involved in post-war efforts at reconciliation. Winkler worked in a coal mine in Mizumaki, a town in Fukuoka prefecture (not to be confused with the Fukuoka camp in Nagasaki). He was part of a group of one thousand Dutch (undoubtedly including 'Indonesians'), British and Australian POWs. Having gained his release, on 22 September he travelled to Nagasaki where he observed first-hand the destruction wreaked by the atomic bomb. Agonizing over his experience, he made a first return visit to Japan in 1985 with a view to striking a sense of reconciliation with his former captors. In Mizumaki village Winkler came across a dilapidated and overgrown monument which, with local cooperation, he sought to restore. The Cross Memorial, as the site is now known, commemorates 869 Dutch POWs who died locally or in other parts of Japan during this period.[7]

---

7   Asami Nagai, 'Making peace with the past. How one small town in Kyushu is going out of its way to promote reconciliation between former enemies,' *The Daily Yomiuri* (29 July 2000). See also Dolf Winkler, *My Past Camp 1942–1945* (Emmeloord, 2002).

Schäfer worked in a shipyard near Nagasaki, just over a kilometre from the epicentre; he survived by jumping into a ditch. Nevertheless, he was exposed to radiation and thus a *hibakusha*. From various writings and interviews, both Winkler and Schäfer were convinced that the atomic bombs served as a key test for the United States. In later years, they both questioned the claimed connection between the atomic bombs and the Japanese capitulation, arguing instead that a guarantee offered the Japanese Emperor that he would not be prosecuted would have been sufficient. With great pathos, Schäfer describes the devastation wreaked by the atomic bomb, including the large number of victims. Critical of the Dutch suppression of the Indonesian independence movement which he saw first-hand in colonial service, in later life he would also critique the US role in Vietnam. No doubt novel in its time, through 1981–82 he published a series of articles in the Japan Communist Party (JCP) newspaper, *Akahata*, later published as a book in Japanese describing his experience as a Dutch *hibakusha*.

Chapter 5

Nagasaki, Japan and Global Peace Movements

A round the world a 'peace movement' would develop, as with Lord Russell's 'ban the bomb' campaign and the emergence of popular or citizens movements to establish nuclear-free zones and municipalities, more or less as predicted by Burchett. In the late 1960s and early 1970s, such movements would coalesce around growing global opposition to the US war in Vietnam, including its strikingly radical Japanese component, especially but not exclusively among the student population. *Hibakusha* had already entered the English vocabulary – indeed even an Oxford dictionary entry – and the widespread anti-nuclear slogan 'No more *hibakusha*' further stretched the original meaning of the term. Obviously this subject is large in consideration of time frame, national and other considerations, just as the potential for additional stretching is considerable, especially when plausibly related issues such as anti-uranium mining or export protests in Australia, actions by Pacific Ocean nations against French nuclear testing, North American and European tangents, and even contemporary Japanese considerations are brought into focus.

The Japan Council against Atomic and Hydrogen Bombs (Gensuikyo)

In Japan, the birth of the Japan Council against Atomic and Hydrogen Bombs (Gensuikyo) coincided with British preparations for nuclear tests in Maralinga in Australia, and Gensuikyo was among those warning the Australian prime minister at the time. Taking the form of a letter of 14 July 1956,[1] Gensuikyo was then in preparation for its second world conference and the staging of mass rallies in Nagasaki and Tokyo. Founded in Japan on 19 September 1955, Gensuikyo is a federated body of 60 national organizations, including youth, women, labour, medical institutions and others with a combined membership of 2.5 million. There are Gensuikyo organizations in all of Japan's 47 prefectures. While Gensuikyo may have gained the backing of communist and socialist-affiliated unions in the past, its approach is non-partisan and represents a rainbow group of activists. Active unto this day, in 2012 Gensuikyo was granted special consultative status with the UN Economic and Social Affairs Council (ECOSOC).

The Anti-War Anti-Base Movement

From a Japanese perspective, opposition to America's war in Vietnam along with the Japan–US Security Treaty gave way in the 1960s and '70s to unprecedented civil society actions backed by the opposition parties, especially the Japan Socialist Party (JSP) and the JCP along with affiliated trade unions and, no less, strident university students and other sections of civil society under the umbrella of the anti-war movement. In particular, the many US bases in Japan became protest targets.

The US Naval base in Sasebo in Nagasaki is a case in point. As the closest feasible target in Japan for North Korean missiles, as

---

1   National Archives of Australia (NAA) A462 449/2 Part 3.

became evident during the crisis of 2017–18, the vulnerability of the base as a target of attack is obvious, just as the base has been upgraded in recent years in line with its strategic importance. When the USS *Enterprise* visited Sasebo in January 1968, the port became a focal point for protests against turning it into a 'nuclear base'.[2] Similarly, and as local opponents of the Japan–US Security Treaty pointed out with respect to a port visit on 27 February 2009 of the US nuclear-powered aircraft carrier *John C. Stennis,* it was most likely carrying nuclear weapons and was thus unwelcome. JCP House of Representatives member Akamine Seiken warned at the time that the US was seeking to use the whole of Kyushu including Sasebo as a staging area for its preemptive attack strategy. There was also a concern that, contrary to constitutional provisions, US forces were conducting joint training exercises with Japanese 'Self-Defense Forces'. Reflecting the JCP position, he also called for a revision of the 'subservient Japan–US alliance'. A rally adopted a resolution calling for a Sasebo City without nuclear weapons and US bases.[3]

After some years of quiescence and with the virtual collapse of the organized left around the Socialist Party, the major locus of the anti-base movement today is Okinawa prefecture in Japan's far south, where civil society groups vent their opposition to the national government's support for construction of a US helipad base. As the only political party calling for the abolition of the Japan–US Security Treaty (as

2   Thomas R. H. Havens, *Fire Across the Sea: The Vietnam War and Japan 1965–1975,* (Princeton, NJ: Princeton University Press, 1987), 146. Also a point noted on a panel at the Nagasaki Atomic Bomb Museum.

3   Japan Press, 'Sasebo residents protest against U.S. nuclear-powered aircraft carrier's visit,' *Akahata,* 1 & 2 March 2009.

revised under Primer Minister Kishi in January 1960), the JCP retains its political force in prefectural elections – as in Okinawa – despite its relatively minor impact at the national level. This is at a time when the government of Abe Shinzo (2006–07; 2012–present) has gone further than conservative predecessors in calling for 'collective defence', a revision of the 'peace constitution', stepped up rocket and missile development, the launching of independent intelligence gathering, the introduction of a widely-critiqued subversion act in 2018, and the strong-handed repression of the anti-US bases movement on Okinawa.[4]

Although US Air Force photographs of nuclear weapons on Okinawa have been publicly available for over 25 years, it was only in February 2016 that the US government officially declassified the fact.[5] As McNeil interprets, Japan's no-nuke rule was undermined by a backroom deal struck between Washington and Tokyo, signed by Japanese Prime Minister Sato Eisaku and US President Richard Nixon in 1969. Although officially denied on both sides of the Pacific, the deal allowed the presence of nuclear-armed US ships and aircraft in or over Japanese territory. In February 2016, Washington finally admitted what had almost become an open secret: nuclear weapons had been stored in Okinawa prior to its reversion to Japanese rule in May 1972. The

---

4   See Gavan McCormack, 'Japan: Prime Minister Abe Shinzo's Agenda,' *The Asia-Pacific Journal | Japan Focus* (Vol. 14, Issue 24, No. 1, 15 December 2016).

5   National Security Archive. Among the photos released by the National Security Archive in 2016 are depictions of Air Force operations in Okinawa, including little-known pictures of US nuclear bombs deployed there during the 1960s.

secret agreement allowed for their re-introduction without prior Japanese consent in times of crisis.[6] Although an open secret for decades, the subject has been controversial because Japan's leaders and US officials have consistently denied the presence of such weapons on Japanese territory.

China's 'Aggressive War' Perspective

Alongside unrepentant discourses on righteous war that strike major resonance among most Japanese, there is also another side of Japanese opinion has gone as far as offering sincerely-felt apologies, especially to Asian victims. Emperor Akihito, who succeeded the Chrysanthemum Throne upon the death of his father in 1989, is on this side, which also includes a number of political figures mostly but not exclusively from the left spectrum of the political field. Some intellectuals, including Ken'ichi Goto, are prepared to concede a 'clash of empire' perspective on the war. In this view, Japanese, British, Americans and Dutch came into a collision course over markets and resources as with an intra-imperialist war that would see the stronger replace the weaker. Followers of this line of thinking may or may not accept the Tokyo Trials judgments, where arraignment of A, B and C war criminals has been deemed by many in Japan as a version of 'victor's justice'. But looking around, it is far harder to find vocal Japanese spokespersons actually coming out to decry Japan's war in China as a war of aggression.

---

6   David McNeil, 'Strategic approach: Washington's shifting nuclear policy in the Asia-Pacific region is putting Japan in a difficult position,' *The Japan Times* (30 July 2017).

Rather, the 'Japan as aggressor in Asia' view comes most strongly from the nation that suffered the most, namely China. The invasion of Korea of course predated the Pacific War and many Koreans shared the fate of other victims of Japan's wartime aggression, whether China, Indochina, the Philippines, Malaya, the former Dutch East Indies, etc.

An article from Xinhua on the occasion of the 71st anniversary of atomic bombing may be seen as representative of the Chinese view.[7] The 2016 edition of this annual commemoration in Tokyo was described as once again 'short of any apology to Japan's neighbours for the war crimes committed by the Imperial Japanese Army and also without any reflection on Japan's militarist history of invasion.' For the reader's edification, the article lectured, 'Japan was a major aggressor that launched wars of aggression against China, Southeast Asian countries and the United States in the 1930s and 1940s.' In an aside on victimhood, the article continued, 'Reflecting on the Hiroshima and Nagasaki tragedy, Tokyo has always focused on Japan's much-trumpeted victimhood, evading the fact that the root cause of the U.S. bombings lies in Japan's militaristic aggression and brutal violence against other countries.' The article reported that 'Tomihisa Taue, mayor of Nagasaki city, urged the government to enshrine into law its Three Non-Nuclear Principles of not possessing, not producing and not permitting the introduction of nuclear weapons on its soil' and then lamented the fact that Taue's voice was drowned out by Prime Minister Abe, 'the revisionist premier and also a hawkish nationalist, [who]

7   Xinhua, 'Nagasaki marks 71st anniv. of A-bombing amid calls for reflecting on Japan's aggression history' (8 September 2016).

also attended the ceremony and delivered a speech', albeit with voices calling for his ouster heard in the background. In a factual aside, Xinhua continued, 'Abe did not mention the historical background and root cause of the atomic bombings, nor did he offer an apology for the war atrocities committed by the Imperial Japanese Army.' In a political aside on then-current politics, the report continued, 'The Abe administration rolled out policies including security bills which might trigger wars, adopted a hostile attitude to some Asian countries including China and hyped up "threat theory" and "sense of crisis" in order to seek excuse for war preparations.' Referring to Japan's plutonium stockpile, a Japanese citizen was quoted as saying, 'Japan's intention to produce nuclear weapons is absolutely clear despite the Abe administration's claim to abandon nuclear weapons.' This was prior to the Korean crisis of 2017–18.

In a commenting upon Japan's school curriculum version of history, the Xinhua article cited an informant's declaration that

> Japanese schools do not tell students about it, Japanese media, meanwhile, focuses on the suffering of Japan in the war. As a result, most Japanese do not know the country's militarist history of invasion. Many Japanese know Japan suffered a lot in the wars, but don't know its Asian neighbours were victimized by Japan's brutal aggression and colonial rule.

This is factual – and put to test in the Japanese university classroom by myself across hundreds of lectures and student reports. In reality, knowledge of this dark period of Japanese history would indeed have to be gained outside

of the educational curriculum. Citing another voice, Abe
is condemned in the Xinhua report for his historical
revisionism. As asserted, 'millions of people in Asia died in
wars waged by Japan and the real reason for [the] Nagasaki
tragedy lies in the war of aggression.' Noting that Japan
had 'adhered to its post-war tradition of pacifism to avoid
mistakes in future', as claimed, it was also true that Abe was
doing exactly the opposite.

Soviet/Russian Takes

Making propaganda from the US nuclear bombings, the
Soviet Union adroitly pursued its own 'peace' discourse
through the Cold War, as with hosting conferences and other
activities, no doubt seductive to true believers, including
many in Japan who interpreted the West as a threatening
enemy. In Nagasaki's Peace Park we can see graphic evidence
of such memorialization. Today, Russia stands against for-
getting the moral side of the atomic bombings of Hiroshima
and Nagasaki. As reported in the *Asahi Shimbun*, Valentina
Matvienko, the head of Russia's upper chamber of Parliament
and reportedly close to Russian President Vladimir Putin,
arrived in Tokyo on 31 October 2016 by invitation of the
Japanese Upper House. This was the first time a high-ranking
Russian government official had visited Nagasaki since Soviet
President Mikhail Gorbachev did so in 1991. After visiting
the museum, Matvienko told Nagasaki Mayor Taue, 'It was
utterly unnecessary to drop atomic bombs [on the Japanese
cities]' . . . . 'It was not hard to estimate how many civilians
would be killed. I think the U.S. just wanted to experiment.'

In December 2014, Sergey Naryshkin, speaker of Russia's lower house of parliament, denounced the atomic bombing of Hiroshima and Nagasaki as crimes against humanity after the US condemned Russia over the situation in Ukraine. Reportedly, Naryshkin said on 4 August 2016 at a session at the Rosatom state atomic energy corporation devoted to the anniversary of Hiroshima and Nagasaki nuclear bombings, 'This barbaric, cynical crime against civilians, which was not in any way justified from the military point of view, should be classified as a crime against humanity that has no expiration date. However, it has still not been properly legally assessed.' As he elaborated, the bombs' purpose was to speed up Japan's capitulation. He also noted that the attacks on Hiroshima and Nagasaki are the only examples of combat use of nuclear weapons in human history. Addressing students at the Moscow State Institute of International Relations, Naryshkin said an international tribunal should be set up to prosecute those responsible for the atomic bombings in August 1945. As he added, the 'bombings were not only aimed at persuading Japan to surrender, but also to warn the USSR, which was America's ally at the time.'

According to Alexander Iliyshev-Vvedenskiy, an official with the Japan division in the Russian Foreign Ministry, documents exist to show that 'there was a real chance to stop the war' before the bombings. Moreover, Japan had already agreed to surrender on the terms described in the Potsdam Declaration. As he further pointed out, on the day of the first bombing, the Japanese Foreign Minister had agreed to surrender on the Soviet Union's terms, and that this information 'probably reached' the Americans. Accordingly, he asserted, this knowledge may have hastened the US decision to drop the atomic bombs. The Russian Foreign Ministry has maintained that the bombings were in violation of the Potsdam Declaration, which called for an end to attacks on civilians.[8]

The Russian interest in Nagasaki came at a time when the city sought to woo other world leaders to visit. Among them was German President Joachim Gauck, who visited on 19 November 2016. Meeting such individuals as senior Nihon Hidankyo official Taniguchi Sumiteru, as Gauck made it known, the dropping of the atomic bomb in Nagasaki was 'completely unnecessary', adding that the brutal atomic destruction presents a warning for people today, because 'Even a democracy is capable of such things.'

---

8   Sinelschikova, 'International tribunal should prosecute perpetrators of Hiroshima.' In the same year a first-hand Soviet report on the Nagasaki bomb also came to hand and placed on the website of the Russian Historical Society. As Ilyshev-Vvedensky commented, this was the first eyewitness account of the horrors of bombardments and what was rightly called a 'crime against humanity.' See TASS. 'Russia publishes unique 1945 Soviet embassy report of Hiroshima bombing' (6 August 2015).

Chapter 6

Memory and Memorialization

$\mathbb{P}$ art of Nagasaki's outreach has been to promote the memorialization of the disaster globally, and city officials are undoubtedly tireless in addressing city-level calls for replica bells etc., the lending of museum exhibits, or promoting official visits and exchanges under the 'peace' banner.[1] For pilgrims to the site of the dropping of the second atomic bomb, the Nagasaki Atomic Bomb Museum and adjacent National Peace Memorial Hall for the Atomic Bomb Victims have become must-visit sites, and hundreds of thousands have done just that. As the Memorial Hall website states:

> We vow to convey the reality of the atomic bomb damages to people both in Japan and abroad, to inform future generations, to learn from history and to build a peaceful world free from nuclear weapons.

Still, it should be remembered, alongside at least 50 'peace' museums in Japan are several that unapologetically eulogize Japan's invasion of China, and even museums dedicated to kamikaze pilots. Many who visit the Nagasaki Museum and Memorial Hall will make comparisons with the Hiroshima Peace Memorial Museum. The Nagasaki version is newer, a pleasingly modern design but more constricted in space. It replaced an earlier version dubbed Rokkakudo, a hexagonal

---

1   For example see the website of Peace Monuments, '26 Monuments Related to Nagasaki: But Not In Nagasaki (Japan).'

building erected adjacent the hypocentre in May 1949. The present version is complementary to the Hiroshima version but with subtly significant differences. Notably, it is shorter on local history than the Hiroshima version, but longer on the science behind the bomb as well as the reality of proliferation and the dangers it imposes.

Entering the Museum one is soon immersed in a salon rather crowded with objects and photographs revealing the awesome destruction of the bomb perhaps with more attention placed upon steel and concrete as with the reassembled section of twisted girders of the Mitsubishi steel plant or concrete steps of a primary school. One will observe near the entrance an assemblage of the ruins of the Urakami Cathedral, and an enlarged photo montage. Few who view it have an inkling as to the politics behind its final destruction. Even as presented, the school children who also pass these halls seem to be turned off by the display along with images of corpses clogging rivers – their silences are sometimes all too palpable. As mentioned, a prominent section of the museum is dedicated to Nagai Takeshi. Copies of his Japanese books are displayed along with various mementoes, letters and other memorabilia.

A little to the side, a large, beautifully designed wall panel offers a diorama of Japanese military actions and entanglements in China starting with the 'Manchurian incident' or the Japanese seizure of the Manchurian city of Mukden (now Shenyang) on 18 September 1931 down unto to surrender. Videos of nine thematic elements related to the war can be accessed, as with the Greater East Asia Co-prosperity Sphere,

Figure 8. "The Age of Militarism": The Manchurian Incident, 1931. (Source: screen grab by author of contested video display, Nagasaki Peace Museum)

the Pacific War, the War against China, etc. The Museum has also incorporated into its video collection the oral narratives of non-Japanese survivors, including forced labourers from Korea and China, along with Australian POWs. Two of the Australian POWs graphically give voice to ritual beatings by rifle butts. One alludes to a baseball bat-wielding bully. Separately, two of them (including Chick), agree on balance that the atomic bombing was good insofar as it ended the war or expedited the end. These videos come across in audible English in a well-traversed section of the museum but, from observation, do not attract a Japanese audience.

Unlike the Hiroshima Peace Memorial Museum, there is no particular statement in the Nagasaki Museum as to the role of the port city's shipyards and munition works as a base for Japanese aggression, even though Nagasaki steelworks is highlighted as a target. While a dedicated exhibit graphically showcases global nuclear proliferation, even counting nuclear warhead stockpiles by nation, there is no particular statement on Japan's own plutonium stockpiles, which are sufficient to fuel hundreds of atomic bombs. Neither is there any particular statement in the Nagasaki Museum on the 'atoms for peace' narrative that led to the nation's acceptance of civilian nuclear power industry nor, for that matter, any explanation of the risks as demonstrated with the Fukushima meltdown.

Over the years I have followed with interest a small corner of the museum reserved for videos of scenes of Japan's war in the Pacific and its invasion of China. The format and contact of these videos has changed over the years, especially with respect to depictions of Nanjing and the infamous massacre perpetrated by Japanese forces of late

1937–early 1938. In 1996, as Laura Hein and Takenaka Kiko explain, alarmed by these changes Japanese conservative nationalist groups went on a counter-offensive. These groups, such as the Liberal View of History Study Group (*Jiyushugi shikan kenkyukai*), led by Fujioka Nobukatsu, had earlier attacked middle-school textbooks as 'self-flagellating' and sought not only to end criticism of Japan's wars of aggression in the 1930s and 1940s but also to swing public opinion in favour of future rearmament. They attacked the Nagasaki Museum curators' plan to 'include in their exhibit' photographs of 'the Nanjing Massacre, Unit 731 and their experiments with biological weapons, and the comfort women'. In response, the Nagasaki Museum removed some pieces from the new exhibit. A video on China, later restored, met with protest from the Chinese consulate in Nagasaki as inappropriate, leading to much internal debate in City Hall on how to respond. Modifications were made and, following a further protest, still more modifications were carried out. Today, the Nanjing massacre is featured matter-of-factly, as are the Japanese army's activities in Manchuria and even its biological experiments on human beings. In any case, about two dozen grainy videos last no more than two minutes each. Seldom have I observed the crowds that surge through the museum even bothering to visit this corner. Although since replaced or modified, the large wall panel of Japan's military surge or rampage through Asia did add some colour and was even met with awe by a public untutored on this facet of Japan's recent past.

Peace Park Observations

Nagasaki's Peace Park presents a picturesquely landscaped space carved out of elevated ground with sweeping views of the port city's verdant and encircling hills. Here stands the iconic 10-metre high Nagasaki Peace Statue, created by a local sculptor and serving as a backdrop to annual speeches and celebratory events. As one enters the park (now rising by escalator) an enfilade of ageing and newer 'peace' statues come into view. Some 100 metres north of the atomic bomb hypocentre, the site straddles the grounds of the former wartime branch of Nagasaki's prison. As adverted, 134 people, staff and inmates (including 32 Chinese and at least 13 Koreans) died here. The sparse remaining mosaic of concrete and brickwork offers a stark reminder of both the prison and its vaporization. Chinese victims of the atomic bombing are commemorated by a newly-installed monument erected by a private group. An inscription states that of the 40,000 Chinese brought to Japan to work in the mining and other industries, 6,830 perished from ill-treatment in just one year. Nagasaki prefecture's coal mines became the workplaces of 1,042 Chinese forced labourers, of whom 32 perished in the prison at the time of the bombing.

Nearby, a set of official monument-sculptures compete for attention. There is one for Brazil, another for Cuba, and yet others for China, Argentina, the Soviet Union, Czechoslovakia and the German Democratic Republic, with the latter trio outliving their former nation state entities and the old Soviet-orchestrated peace discourse they once undoubtedly heralded. There is no official US

Figure 9. Monument to Chinese victims of the atomic bombing, Peace Park, 2018. (Source: author)

monument-sculpture. For its part, India erected a stunning white pagoda or actually Hindu-Buddhistic stupa on a nearby mountaintop. From social realist to modernistic designs, the statues present a striking assemblage. Some are erected by cities but, as with the nation state statues, they seem to be saying that it is we, cities and peoples alongside states, who mediate issues of war and peace, life and death.

An outstanding new entry to the Peace Park, erected in April 2016, taps into a new discourse of international solidarity for *hibakusha*, a select group for sure, albeit expanding if we add the many victims of Chernobyl, Fukushima and many other modern 'peaceful disasters'. Taking the form of an Australian eucalyptus tree trunk with an aboriginal wooden *piti* or carrying dish wedged in a fork, it strikes an odd note. Dubbed 'The Tree of Life: Gift of Peace', it seeks to symbolize the sharing or resources between families, communities, and nations. Gifted by a number of Australian cities along with Anangu aboriginal community leaders, it sends a message of acknowledgement of atomic survivors worldwide, including indigenous Australians, service personnel and their descendants 'affected by British nuclear testing in Australia at Maralinga, Emu Field and Monte Bello islands' (a reference to twelve atmospheric tests conducted in Australia between 1952 and 1957 by the United Kingdom).

Korean Victims

Closer to the Atomic Bomb Museum and therefore not part of the Peace Park gallery sits a lone monument to Korean victims of the atomic bombing. Erected on 9 August 1979, as the English explanation states, 'This monument has been dedicated to the more than 10,000 Koreans who were victims of the atomic bombing in Nagasaki.' The inscription, signed by the 'Nagasaki Association to Protect Human Rights of Koreans in Japan', explains this is a private memorial erected by a 'group of Japanese' to remember the 'tragic war loss' of the Koreans and to offer an apology for the Japanese colonization of Korea, for 'threatening them with the sword and the gun' and for forcing them into slavery in Japan before meeting such an end. Offering a brief history lesson, the inscription reads:

> On August 22, 1910, the Japanese government put into effect a declaration to annex Korea and to colonize the nation under the strict and complete rule of Japan, Koreans were deprived of life to live as free citizens [obscure] . . . human rights were grossly neglected. Many were driven into Japan having no recourse to live in Korea. The total number of Koreans most of whom were forcibly brought to Japan and put to slavery is believed to have been 2,365,268 according to the Home Ministry. Of these, approximately 70,000 were located in Nagasaki Prefecture just before the Japanese surrender in World War II. At that time over 31,000 Koreans lived in and around the city of Nagasaki and were engaged in forced labour under atrocious conditions.

The inscription continues by explaining that some 20,000 Koreans experienced the bomb and half were instantly killed. The message ends with a call for the 'total abolition of nuclear weapons from the face of the earth' and the 'peaceful unification of the Korean nation' (a position then shared by both Koreas notwithstanding the tense state of armed truce).

Most of Nagasaki's Korean victims, who came from Hapcheon County in South Gyeongsang Province, were forcibly conscripted for labour in wartime factories, including the notorious undersea Hashima coal mines. One cohort of between 600 and 800 Koreans were employed as miners on a tunnel excavation site, part of an underground complex where a branch of the Mitsubishi Arms Factory manufactured aircraft torpedoes. Located on the northern perimeter of the Urakami valley, everyone working underground at the time survived the A-bomb blast. Those recuperating in outside dormitories from 12 hour working shifts, however, almost certainly perished. Korean survivors of the A-bombs returned home after the war to establish an organization similar to the Japan Confederation of A- and H-Bomb Sufferers' Organizations (Hidankyo), and the two organizations maintain close contact.

That is not the end of the story with respect to Korean victims of the atomic bombing. Many Korean atomic bomb sufferers have striven over the decades to win eligibility for pensions granted officially acknowledged Hibakusha. According to a survivors' association, an estimated 30,000 of the 70,000 Koreans in Hiroshima and Nagasaki at the time lived through the bombs. A monument to Korean victims at the peace memorial park in Hiroshima states that about 10 per cent of the 200,000 people lost to the bomb were ethnically Korean.[2] Of the 50,000 who survived, 43,000 returned to what became South Korea, where they suffered from the long-term effects of radiation exposure and many died without receiving proper treatment.

2   Sam Kim, 'Hibakusha of "Korea's Hiroshima" still press for redress' (*The Japan Times,* 6 August 2015).

Figure 10. Mitsubishi Sumiyoshi Tunnel Arms Factory with torpedo missile on display. A six-tunnel complex, each was 300 metres in length. On the day of the bomb, 1,800 people were working here manufacturing precision torpedo parts additional to the 800-1,000 Korean forced labourers conducting tunneling operations. After the bomb the tunnels served to shelter homeless survivors. (Source: author)

Inside Japan, the Koreans continue to face down discrimination and prejudice, legally barred from Japanese citizenship even though many had fought for Japan during the war. People who are both Korean and *hibakusha* face a double prejudice in marriage and employment. From 1967, Koreans began to organize to fight for pension rights, which were more or less granted with the 1995 Supreme Court ruling but only honoured in the breach in the case of many. Other non-Japanese *hibakusha* include those who migrated, as with the case of numerous American-born Japanese in

Japan at the time of the war, but who subsequently returned to the US.[3]

The complexity of the issue is revealed in a report published in the JCP newspaper *Akahata*, which explains how Choi, a Korean survivor of the Nagasaki bomb who later returned to Korea, was denied compensation on the grounds that he resided outside of Japan. Two months before his death in 2004 at the age of 78, Choi filed a lawsuit demanding that the national government and the Nagasaki City government pay a total of 9.6 million yen in health care benefits and compensation. His relatives continued the lawsuit and, in September 2005, won a victory at the Fukuoka High Court. The following November, the Atomic Bomb Survivors Relief Law was revised to allow sufferers residing overseas to apply from abroad for the benefits after Japan has issued a *Hibakusha* certificate.[4]

These stories could be repeated, as with the case of Chick, who received the pension in Australia just two years before his death in 2014 at the age of 92. He is the only Australian POW of the surviving 24 incarcerated at Fukuoka Camp 14-B to be issued a *Hibakusha* certificate. Bill Reed, son of Private William Cecil Reed and another of the 24 Australian POWs, was informed by the Memorial Hall in Nagasaki that a database had been set up to record the names of everyone in the city when the bombing happened. This is undoubtedly a positive step, especially as Reed had spent 18 months

---

3   Susan Southard, *Nagasaki: Life After Nuclear War* (New York: Viking, 2015).

4   Akahata, 'High court overturns order to pay benefits to South Korean Hibakusha' (*Akahata*, 23 January 2007).

tracking down the relatives of the 24 Australians with a view to registering their personal details 'so their presence in Nagasaki would never be lost or forgotten.' Part of Nagasaki's outreach has been to promote the memorialization of the disaster globally and city officials are undoubtedly tireless, as intimated, in addressing city-level calls for the lending of museum exhibits, or official visits and exchanges under the 'peace' banner.

POW Memorialization

Set up in March 2002, the POW Research Network Japan held its 1st Annual Meeting in Tokyo, inter alia coordinating, publicizing and documenting POW visits to Japan, hitherto mounted on a personal and ad hoc basis. Many sites and cities are targeted and numerous activities touch Nagasaki. Between 10–16 August 2013, an Irish TV crew visited Japan to interview and gather information on Aidan MacCarthy, as discussed above. On 13 September 2015, a memorial monument (a large stone engraved in English and Japanese) was erected at the site of Fukuoka 2B Camp (present Koyagi Middle School) to remember all 73 victims and the ones who survived in the presence of relatives of victims and officials from foreign embassies. Henk Kleijn, a 90-year-old Dutchman, was the only surviving POW present at the event. Another monument was erected for a B-29 crew killed in a crash in the mountains near the Camp while airdropping relief supplies immediately after the war.

Contested Display: The Negative Response to the Dutch Exhibition by Public Peace Museums

In 2000 Japan and the Netherlands celebrated the 400th anniversary of their relations such as conducted at Nagasaki by hosting various cultural, scientific, economic and sporting events throughout the country. On this occasion, the Netherlands Institute for War Documentation created an exhibition to promote mutual understanding about wartime experiences. Convened by Dr Erik Somers, the exhibition chronicled the experiences of Dutch, Japanese and local people during the Japanese occupation of the former Dutch East Indies. With the exhibit touring Japan in 2000 and 2001, it was first offered to public museums including the Hiroshima Peace Memorial Museum and Nagasaki Atomic Bomb Museum, but rejected by all. In the event, the Dutch exhibition was shown at a small number of private museums and venues including Shiminkaikan (Citizens' Hall) in Nagasaki from 16 to 24 November 2000 through the efforts of the Nagasaki Peace Institute. I was a participant in this symposium along with Japanese peace researcher Yamane Kazuyo and others.

Yamane Kazuyo explained that in the latter half of the 1990s, as public peace museums finally began to stage exhibits on Japanese aggression, they also began to face down attacks by right-wingers. From 1996 onwards, nationalists repeatedly attacked the Nagasaki Atomic Bomb Museum, claiming that 'exhibits on Japanese aggression and invasion would lead to justifying the U.S. atomic bombing.' In essence, the museum had become the face of initiatives by the Ministry of Education that sought to offer more balance on Japan's invasion of China. Yamane pointed out that these attacks conformed to a characteristic pattern among nationalists: to deny Japan's aggression in order to glorify World War II, or to justify the war as an attempt to liberate Asian countries from European colonialism. They refuse to admit that one of the consequences of Japan's aggression was the use of the atomic bombs by the United States. They insist that the reason why the United States dropped an atomic bomb on Hiroshima was 'not to destroy Hiroshima which had developed as the militarily important city, but to test the power of an atomic bomb.' As Yamane explained, public peace museums refused to host the Dutch exhibition because its depictions of Japanese aggression would provoke right-wingers to attack it. As she came to understand (and as China invariably complains), Japanese are ignorant of modern history, especially their nation's aggression towards other countries during the war. Moreover, even if students have an interest in this history, Japan's wartime aggression is often not covered at high school because 'the general history tends to be taught without referring to World War II.'[5]

Museum Observations

I mentioned above that Soviet researchers rushed to document and analyze the effects of the bombs. Their data

5   Yamane Kazuyo, 'Controversial Exhibitions at Peace Museums in Japan,' *Ritsumeikan Kokusai-kenkyu* (vol. 18, no.3, March 2006, 473–86). On a visit to the Nagasaki Atomic Bomb Museum in July 2018, I witnessed a neo-nationalist 'attack.' This took the form of a speaker van parked adjacent the Museum blasting a high-decibel rant combined with raucous Buddhist-themed music, presumably to present patriotic credentials.

had been closely held until 4 August 2016 when Sergey Naryshkin, chairman of the Russian Duma, presented footage documenting the devastation of Hiroshima and Nagasaki to Prime Minister Abe Shinzo. The footage was immediately released to Japanese media and one day later the Nagasaki Atomic Bomb Museum started showing the moving images in its feature exhibition gallery. Believed to have been shot on 16 September 1945, it is the second-earliest known film of the destroyed city, after the one taken by the US military on 8 and 9 September 1945. Besides showing concerned Soviet researchers in the field, the film also reveals the scale of damage inflicted upon industrial facilities in Nagasaki, including the Mitsubishi Steel Manufacturing Company and a torpedo factory.[6]

The Urakami Cathedral Debate

Icons to wartime destruction can have a powerful effect upon subsequent memories and interpretations. Few pack the emotional punch of Hiroshima's Atomic Dome, originally an Industrial Promotion Hall, but Berlin's Kaiser Wilhelm Memorial Church and Auschwitz can be mentioned in the same breath. Issues of memorialization emerged early on in Nagasaki and the surviving ruins of Urakami Cathedral became a highly contested site, not only locally (as registered in City Hall debates) but with the US also showing its hand. In March 1958, the remnants of the cathedral were demolished and, in the following year, a new cathedral was erected

---

6   Yosuke Takashima and Kentaro Yamano, 'Hiroshima, Nagasaki release Soviet footage of A-bomb damage' (*The Asahi Shimbun*, 5 August 2016).

in a more modern style that left practically no trace of the original. The contrast between the demolition and rebuilding of Urakami Cathedral and the preservation of Hiroshima's Atomic Dome could not be greater.

As explained by Otsuki Tomoe, the dismantling of the ruins of the Urakami Cathedral faced strong opposition from Nagasaki residents, including *hibakusha*. From his inauguration in 1951 until 1956, Nagasaki mayor Tagawa Tsutomu sought to ensure the preservation of the ruins, in line with the will of many Nagasaki residents. However, according to Otsuki, in 1955, Tagawa entered into a process at American invitation to formulate a sister-city relationship between Nagasaki and St. Paul, sealed when the mayor visited the United States in August 1956. According to Otsuki, after his return from the US, Tagawa became reluctant to comply with the committee's recommendation for the preservation of the ruins. As Otsuki reasonably argues, American policymakers may have been apprehensive about the potential that the cathedral ruins could serve as a pilgrimage site or an icon of an international anti-nuclear movement.

As Otsuki continues, the priest-custodian urged by the Urakami Catholic community to preserve the ruins characterized them as 'trash'. Accordingly, in February 1958, it was announced that dismantlement of the ruins would commence within the month. Meantime, a local newspaper reported that Mayor Tagawa described the dismantling as 'unavoidable', although committee members of the Atomic Bomb Material Preservation along with Nagasaki councilmen rejected that characterization. In the event, construction of the new

Urakami Cathedral was completed in October 1959. Three statues that had survived the bombing were placed in front of the new cathedral, with a portion of the wall relocated and positioned adjacent the epicentre site in the Nagasaki Peace Park. As Otsuki points out, while Urakami Catholic leaders described the new cathedral as a symbol of the recovery and reconstruction of their community, Nagasaki lost, in perpetuity and lamentably, its most powerful symbol of 'the dawn and suffering of the nuclear age'.

Buddhist Memorials

Setting aside the considerable sizable Catholic community in A-bombed Nagasaki, we should not neglect the fact that the majority of victims were actually part of a broader Shintoist-Buddhist religious tradition. A fact not lost upon local believers is that Nagasaki's major Shinto shrine (Suwa-jinja) located in the Nishiyama precinct was spared destruction and thus deemed protected by the *kami* or gods. Dating back to 1624 and coinciding with the first major wave of Christian persecutions, the construction of Suwa-jinja coincided with waves of Obaku or Zen Buddhist monks, who arrived in Nagasaki along with Chinese traders loyal to the beleaguered Southern Ming (then facing attack from invading Manchu forces) and set up monastic communities around three so-called *fuku* temples. Two splendidly survive, but not the oldest and largest: the Fukusai temple, founded in 1628. Hugging the hillside more or less adjacent Nagasaki station and therefore exposed to the full blast and/or fireball effect of the bomb, hardly a stone remains of this former national treasure. Today rebuilt in the form of a giant Goddess of Mercy astride a no less giant turtle, a single notice in English proclaims 'total destruction by atomic bomb in August 1945'. From the heights of the Goddess statue, a suspended Foucault pendulum – remarkable in itself – draws attention to the basement of the turtle-temple. There, alongside several cases of molten glass and burnt tiles, resides a mini-museum exhibiting Japanese Imperial Army military paraphernalia, including uniforms, an officer's leather boots, signed battalion flags, ammunition, naval shell casings and even a rusty sub-machine gun retrieved from Saipan. Between war and peace, science and religion, the message is certainly mixed, but only Buddhist temple cognoscenti would even discover this place, as it is well off the tourist circuit.

The Oka Masaharu Memorial Museum

Nagasaki also hosts the private Oka Masaharu Memorial Peace Museum. Located a stone's throw from the infamous grounds where 26 Christian martyrs were executed at the end of the sixteenth century – a veritable Catholic pilgrim's site – the museum offers an unambiguous take on Japan's wartime aggression. Oka Masaharu was a Protestant minister, member of the city assembly and representative of the protest group on Rights of Koreans in Nagasaki. According to a museum pamphlet, its purpose is to 'reveal the reality of aggression by the Japanese army' and to demand 'honest apologies' from the Japanese government along with 'proper' compensation for the victims. With the exception of a thematic display on Korean atomic bomb survivors, the museum is not focused specifically upon the atomic bombing of Nagasaki, which is matched with corresponding thematic displays on forced labour, aggression in Korea and China, 'the truth of the sphere of co-prosperity in East Asia' and the Japanese army's sex slavery. It is thus deliberately pitched at Japan's historic war crimes reaching back to the invasion and colonization of Korea. Embellished with graphic photos and exhibits, the museum offers an in-your-face experience guaranteed to shock and awe. During my visit, a group of young women were actually in tears (Koreans or Japanese, I didn't ask). With its tri-lingual Japanese, Korean and English explanations and photo-captions, all grammar-perfect, the museum clearly seeks outreach. Neither is it backward looking: a section is devoted to newspaper clippings relating to the actions of the current Japanese government in diluting the peace constitution and rearming in other ways that evoke memories of the tragic past.

Chapter 7

The Nagasaki City Hall
Peace Discourse

The office of the mayor in Nagasaki has always been controversial, at least as presented in the news and sometimes for the wrong reasons. This office is the subject of a full chapter of Norma Field's celebrated study of memory and the role of the Emperor in post-war Japan. Moreover, public expectation is high that the office of the mayor will vigorously defend Nagasaki's unique history as an atomic-bombed city and the last such city to suffer this fate. Mayors are frequently seen hosting international peace or disarmament conferences and attending high profile events abroad, sometimes in defiance or at cross-purposes with the political line hewed in Tokyo. Nagasaki City Hall can count a number of achievements and initiatives over the years, not only in maintaining its celebrated Atomic Bomb Museum since it opened in 1949 but also, for example, for the Nagasaki Peace Charter, essentially a pacifist document memorized by generations of local school children since it was launched on 27 March 1989. No less significant, and on every 9th August since 1948, the Nagasaki mayor presides over a commemoration ceremony held in the Peace Park precinct, attended by citizens, government officials, atomic bomb survivors along with ambassadors and other foreign dignitaries. On this occasion, the mayor solemnly reads a Peace Declaration. A minute of silence is observed at 11:02 a.m., the time the atomic bomb exploded over this city. As in 2018, I was an informal attendee along with a mixed group of city folk who thronged outside the official visitor's tent, and can so attest this is a prayerful moment. My time in Nagasaki has overlapped with three mayors, namely Motoshima Hitoshi who served four terms as mayor of Nagasaki from 1979 to 1995; Ito Iccho in office from May 1995–April 2007; and the incumbent as I write, Taue Tomihisa. The following focuses upon these three individuals. The first and last of these made indelible marks on Nagasaki as a city of nuclear peace.

Surely the most sensational event surrounding the office of mayor occurred in 1990 when, on 18 January, a pistol-wielding rightist shot Mayor Motoshima Hitoshi in the back. Miraculously he survived. Born in the Goto Islands of Nagasaki prefecture, he was orphaned as a child and brought up as a Catholic by his grandparents. At the age of 21 he was conscripted into the Japanese Imperial Army as an artilleryman, remaining in Japan and never seeing action. Not actually a *hibakusha*, Motoshima was in neighbouring Kumamoto prefecture at the time of the A-bombing. Working in Nagasaki as a teacher before entering politics, he was elected to the prefectural legislature under the LDP banner (but subsequently dumped). At a city meeting in December 1988, he was asked by a JCP member about the Emperor's war responsibility. Reportedly he replied:

> If I look at the descriptions in Japanese and foreign histories, and reflect on my experiences in the military in the education training of soldiers, in that regard I think the Emperor has war responsibility. But based on the will of

a majority of Japanese and Allied countries, the Emperor escaped and became a symbol in the new Constitution, and we have to act under that understanding.[1]

As the late mayor told journalist-literateur Ian Buruma long after the event,

> Forty-three years have passed since the end of the war, and I think we have had enough chance to reflect on the nature of the war. From reading various accounts from abroad and having been a soldier myself, involved in military education, I do believe that the emperor bore responsibility for the war . . . .

In an interview with Bryan Covert in *Kyoto Journal,* Motoshima acknowledged that there were other reasons behind the shooting than just his remarks about the emperor's war responsibility; namely his support for employing foreign people at Nagasaki City Hall, his position on discrimination towards women, his position on openness to accepting refugees, and his willingness to apologize to Koreans over wartime treatment. As he summed up, 'I made all those comments one right after another, so I think that caused the shooting'. Although I met the late mayor by coincidence at the local airport, it was not the right time or place to discuss this issue.

Backed by the LDP, Itoh Iccho first took office in 1995. A Waseda University graduate, he majored in political science. Among other acts commensurate with the city's history, he

1   David E. Sanger, 'Special to The New York Times, Mayor Who Faulted Hirohito Is Shot' (*The New York Times*, 19 January 1990).

made a speech at the International Court of Justice in The Hague on 7 November 1995, inter alia stressing that the use of nuclear weapons was a violation of international law. Meeting Itoh at a UN disarmament conference in Nagasaki which the city co-hosted, he appeared comfortable in this role and was certainly gregarious as befits a host of an international meeting. As with his predecessors and successors, his role as Nagasaki mayor was simply to defend the nuclear disarmament cause and to showcase to the world the suffering that befalls victims of atomic radiation as in Nagasaki. On 17 April 2007, while campaigning for re-election for his fourth term, he was shot twice in the back at point-blank range in front of his campaign office outside the Nagasaki station. Itoh died early the next morning due to loss of blood. Police arrested a senior member of the Yamaguchi-gumi crime group, well represented in Nagasaki. As I then learned from local informants, although the yakuza assailant certainly had links with right-wing political groups, the motive for his killing was not analogous to the attempt on Motoshima. Itoh had been a leading member of a circle of Kyushu (Island)-based mayors tasked to root out corruption at a time when Yamaguchi-gumi was understood to be favoured in local Nagasaki construction contracts. According to rumour, the assassin bridled at the prospect of being shut out and took revenge upon Itoh. The Nagasaki District Court sentenced the accused to death on 26 May 2008, but the Fukuoka High Court later commuted the sentence to life in prison.

Itoh's assassination so close to the day of the 2007 mayoral election vote virtually creating a national legal crisis; some of the early ballots had already been cast and the electoral law hastily amended by the Japanese Diet. Itoh's widow declined candidacy. His son-in-law, a journalist for the *Asahi* newspaper, joined the race only to be narrowly defeated by the admittedly capable and personable City Hall bureaucrat Taue Tomihisa. Bureaucrats are as widely revered in Japan as they are disdained in many other countries. Mayor Taue has sought to enhance Nagasaki's international outreach in seeking to rid the world of nuclear weapons.

Every August without fail, the Japanese media observes the anniversary of the end of World War II with retrospective pieces, especially recalling the atomic bombings. In Nagasaki at the exact moment on the anniversary of the dropping of the bomb, strategically placed City Hall sirens across the city wail, echoed by the deeper tone of ship klaxons sounding in the harbour. Life comes to a momentary stop. Citizens close their eyes and bow. From even earlier in the morning, school children will dress for the event as people begin to assemble along with visiting dignitaries. The solemn atmosphere is somewhere between high church and an imperial reception. At each annual ceremony, a list of *hibakusha* who died over the previous year is enshrined, and the total number of deaths during and resulting from the Nagasaki atomic bombing is reverently tallied. For example, the 9 August ceremony held in 2018 included the dedication of a list of 3,511 atomic bomb sufferers who had passed away during the previous year including – in a possible display of independence or displeasure – 68 not officially recognized as *Hibakusha* by the central government. This was the first time that Nagasaki City Hall had made this inclusion. On this date, the average age of survivors in Hiroshima and Nagasaki stood at over 82.

Drafting the Nagasaki
City Hall Peace Declaration

Since the practice was first initiated in 1948, the drafting of
the 'peace declaration' address to mark the anniversary of the
atomic bomb attack has been subject to various constraints
and political influences. Obviously, the constraints were
heavy under direct SCAP administration at least through to
1952, as the US sought to script a narrative that would excul-
pate its own role in visiting disaster upon Nagasaki. Catholic
narratives promoting the 'providence of God' may well have
served to ease Nagasaki's sense of victimhood in the early
years, just it would take years for the voices of *hibakusha* to
be heard. More or less, as Hiroshima used its annual peace
declaration to cement its status as a city of 'peace', Nagasaki
took this opportunity to position itself enigmatically as an
'international cultural city'.[2]

In more recent years, drafts of the declaration are worked out
through consensus of a committee made up of city bureaucrats
including the mayor, *hibakusha* representatives and some
outside advisers and senior figures held in community esteem.
Altogether they number more than ten, including until the
present a well-known *hibakusha* woman. Nevertheless it is the
mayor who signs off on the Peace Declaration and reads it on
the occasion of the anniversary of the bombing.

In recent years an exceptional role in the Peace Declaration
Drafting Committee was assigned to former Nagasaki

---

2   Many of these themes are discussed in great detail in Diehl, *Resurrecting
    Nagasaki*, 34–39.

University president Tsuchiyama Hideo (d. 2017) who added a striking pacifist voice not only in opposition to nuclear non-proliferation but also cautioning against Japan's remilitarization. A medical student in Nagasaki, Tsuchiyama headed to Saga Prefecture, where his mother had evacuated, on the morning of the atomic bombing. The following day, he was exposed to radiation after he returned to help victims in Nagasaki. An older brother and his wife died in the atomic bombing. Especially after stepping down from his university post in 1992, he became an important voice in the Nagasaki peace movement. He resigned from his official role in 2016 at the age of 92, although not without critical words about the 2016 declaration which removed a phrase relating to Tokyo's turn away from pacifism and towards redefining the war-renouncing constitution.[3]

In 2014, while Prime Minister Abe Shinzo maneuvered to have Japan's right to 'collective self-defence' approved, Tsuchiyama argued during a Nagasaki Peace Declaration drafting meeting that the declaration from the atomic-bombed city should include words that rein in the national government. His voice evidently prevailed and the final draft of the declaration noted that 'rushed debate over collective self-defense has given rise to the concern.' Furthermore, as the declaration noted, the principle of pacifism was wavering and, accordingly, the government should 'take serious heed of these distressed voices.' In meetings of the Peace Declaration drafting committee for 2015, Tsuchiyama continued to voice his concerns over

---

3   Kato Sayo, 'Hibakusha: Arrogance of runaway gov't could lead to war: ex-Nagasaki Univ. pres.,' *The Mainichi* (16 November 2016).

security-related bills that the government was trying to pass. As he explained to *The Mainichi*,

> The reason I was adamant that the declaration address the bills was because I had the sense that they could open the way for war . . . . Atomic-bombed cities must speak for everyday people who feel a vague sense of anxiety.

As intimated above, this anxiety extended beyond atomic bombs and was now understood by large sections of the population to include a range of risks associated with all things nuclear. The threat of nuclear disaster such as portended by recurrent power plant accidents over the previous decade came home to roost with the Fukushima Daiichi nuclear power plant disaster of 3 March 2011. This is the subject of Chapter 8. Here we limit ourselves to how Nagasaki City Hall engaged in the discussion.

Needless to say, amid widespread community indignation at the handling of the Fukushima power plant disaster and calls to shut down existing plants over safety and other issues, great expectations were locally held that Nagasaki City Hall would strike its own position on the use of civilian nuclear power. In July 2011, Mayor Taue unveiled a draft of the peace declaration, the first in the wake of the disaster, calling for a shift away from dependence on nuclear power generation. Taue said that he felt it was important to reflect upon the Fukushima disaster in that year's message, not only calling for the abolition of all nuclear weapons worldwide, but also for Japan to move toward safer energy sources. Taue revealed that the committee had debated long and hard on how to reflect what happened in Fukushima from the standpoint of a city that suffered an atomic bombing. Meanwhile, as the national broadcaster NHK reported, the panel was divided over whether or not atomic bombs and nuclear power could be viewed in the same way. Some participants said City Hall in Nagasaki had a responsibility to call for a shift away from nuclear power, while others pointed out that a distinction should be made between atomic bombs and nuclear power generation.[4]

An explicit reference to the 3/11 Fukushima disaster appeared in his August 2012 address. Mayor Taue called for a society 'free from the fear of radioactivity.' He was thus the first Japanese mayor to call on Japan to move away from nuclear energy and promote instead new energy sources. Taue also called for action on the radioactive waste that has piled up, and pledged that Nagasaki would 'continue to support the people of Fukushima.'[5] Nevertheless, such warnings have not been explicitly repeated in annual Peace Declarations and neither has the mayor re-entered the civilian nuclear power debate.

In his the 2016 Peace Declaration, Mayor Taue soberly repeated many warnings as to a nuclear apocalypse if the world is not freed of nuclear weapons. With respect to the domestic political agenda of the government headed by Abe Shinzo, he pleaded with Tokyo 'to enshrine the Three Non-Nuclear Principles in law, and create a "Northeast Asia

---

4   Japan Today, 'Nagasaki mayor to refer to Fukushima accident in peace declaration,' *Japan Today* (29 July 2011).

5   AsiaNews.it, 'Nagasaki mayor calls for a nuclear-free world,' AsiaNews.it (8 September 2012).

Nuclear Weapons-Free Zone" as a framework for security that does not rely on nuclear deterrence.[6]

In July 2017, a global ban on nuclear weapons was approved at UN headquarters in New York with a total of 122 countries signing the Treaty on the Prohibition of Nuclear Weapons (although none of the signatories possessed a nuclear bomb). Japan's absence from the talks appalled *hibakusha* spokespersons. The same sense of resolution was also carried in Mayor Taue's 9 August 2017 Peace Declaration issued at a ceremony to mark the 72nd anniversary of the atomic bombing of Nagasaki. The signing of the Treaty, he noted, was 'a moment when all the efforts of the *hibakusha* over the years finally took shape.' However, he lamented, 'the nuclear-armed states are opposed to this treaty and there is no end in sight to the road towards a world free of nuclear weapons, the realization of which is our objective.' As he continued, despite the Japanese government's proclaimed leadership in creating a world free of nuclear weapons, and its bridge-making role between the nuclear and non-nuclear-armed states, its failure to participate in diplomatic negotiations for the Nuclear Prohibition Treaty was incomprehensible to those living in the cities that suffered atomic bombings.

ANOTHER SHADOW LINGERED over the Peace Declaration of 2017, namely the bellicose actions of North Korea, which tested weapons of mass destruction and provocatively flew the missiles designed to carry them over Hokkaido. This behaviour was matched by equally strident rhetoric from US President Donald Trump, who literally threatened a

6   Shohei Okada, 'Nagasaki mayor tells world: Visit to see how nukes affect humans,' *The Asahi Shimbun* (9 August 2016).

Figure 11. Mayor Taue Tomihisa reads the 2018 Nagasaki Peace Declaration at Peace Park. Prime Minister Abe Shinzo and UN Secretary-General António Guterres off-camera. (Source: author)

nuclear exchange. Needless to say, the tense atmosphere fed back to Japanese politics with calls by some politicians to invite the US to re-deploy nuclear weapons in Japan, just as

Japan sought to beef up its own missile defences. Still, the atmosphere of high tension and risk was mitigated by the Panmunjom Declaration of 27 April 2018 by the leaders of North and South Korea, and the first-ever US–North Korea summit, held in Singapore on 12 June 2018 looking ahead to the denuclearization of the Korean peninsula, however disingenuous the rhetoric of this occasion especially given complex issues surrounding verification.

Needless to say, the 2018 declaration commemorating the 73rd anniversary looked back at the previous years' events. Mayor Taue duly noted the 'great expectations' held by the international community for the 'realization of irreversible denuclearization' such as those stemming from the Panmunjom Declaration and the US–North Korea Summit. He also noted that more than 300 local assemblies across Japan had voiced their desire to see the Nuclear Prohibition Treaty signed and ratified. In an oblique reference to Tokyo, he called upon nuclear weapons states and countries dependent on 'nuclear umbrellas' to turn to national security policies not dependent on nuclear weapons. Prime Minister Abe Shinzo, who also spoke at the 9 August ceremony in Nagasaki, failed to even mention the Treaty. UN Secretary-General António Guterres also spoke at the ceremony. In the presence of representatives of the five recognized nuclear weapons states, he asserted that the total elimination of nuclear weapons 'remains the highest disarmament priority of the United Nations.' Lamenting that states in possession of nuclear weapons were spending vast sums to modernize their arsenals, he also praised the *hibakusha* as 'the true messengers of peace' while entering the plea, 'There can be no more Hiroshimas, no more Nagasakis, no more *Hibakusha*'.

Chapter 8

Atoms for Peace and the Fukushima Counternarrative

It has struck some that a country reborn out of the ashes of war and, at the same time invested with – at least one would assume – nuclear allergy could, within decades, grasp nuclear power as an energy option. This is all the more the ironic as a country with a Peace Constitution, three non-nuclear principles and commitment to nuclear disarmament. Across the political spectrum, Japan feigned shock at the *Daigo Fukuryu Maru* or Lucky Dragon incident, a reference to the dangerous exposure to atomic radiation experienced by the crew of a Japanese tuna fishing boat, the *Lucky Dragon*, which strayed into the perimeter of a US nuclear test at Bikini Atoll in the Marshall Islands on 1 March 1954. Dubbed Bravo and staged by a joint Army–Navy task force these were the first atomic explosions since the bombings of Japan a year earlier.[1] Panic ensued when irradiated tuna was sold in Japanese cities and eaten by scores of people. With the crew hospitalized back in Japan and undergoing treatment, the US proved uncooperative in revealing data on the test that might have helped the medical profession. Prime Minister Yoshida

---

1 Documents posted by the National Security Archive about 'Operation Crossroads' shed light on these events as do galleries of declassified videos and photographs. Of two tests staged to determine the effects of the new weapons on warships, the 'Baker test' was the most dangerous: it contaminated nearby test ships and the sailors who manned them with radioactive mist.

Shigeru was well aware that pressing for compensation for the Lucky Dragon victims would not only dampen relations with the US, a priority for his administration, but also risked fanning both anti-US sentiment and a home-grown anti-nuclear movement at the same time. Mass signing of petitions against hydrogen bombs had already kicked off. As recalled in his address to the 73rd anniversary of the atomic bombing on 8 August 2018, Tanaka Terumi, speaking as an atomic bomb survivor representative, the movement led to the creation in August 1956 of the Japan Confederation of A-and H-bomb Sufferers Organizations or Nihon Hidankyo. The following year, the pacifist Buddhist movement Sokka Gaikai began to call for a complete ban on nuclear weapons.

As Otsuki Tomoe points out, not only did the incident heighten Japanese public awareness of and sensitivity to the dangers of nuclear testing, but anti-nuclear sentiment grew rapidly even as Washington sought to minimize the political damage caused by the Bravo test. Undeterred, and even going as far as attacking Japanese critics including the victims, the US continued the Bikini Atoll tests even after the Lucky Dragon incident went public. With Japanese anti-nuclear and anti-American sentiment heightened to an unprecedented degree, the stage was set for the evolution of a national movement calling for a total ban on nuclear tests. Still, the focus of discontent was on nuclear tests and not civilian nuclear power, a distinction that would be avidly grasped by the Japanese science and engineering establishment. We need to how and why and, indeed, how attitudes would change among the general public but only after a cataclysmic event.

'Atoms for Peace' – Japan's Civilian Nuclear Power

Civilian nuclear power (albeit not without military application as with the stockpiling of weapons-grade plutonium) has always been a contested issue in the only country to have suffered the effects of the atomic bomb. Even though, as mentioned, the Tokyo government embraced civilian nuclear power as a hedge on the country's dependence upon foreign sources of energy, siting issues for the nation's 20 or so nuclear reactors have been bitterly contested just as locals were strong-armed or bought off to accept compliance.[2] Notwithstanding trade union and other civil society opposition to the steady development of the nuclear power industry, alarm bells began to be sounded as to poor siting decisions with respect to seismic conditions and with more than one plant suffering damage or proven vulnerable to accident owing to earthquake activity. In the event, the siting of Fukushima Daiichi plant was obviously inappropriate owing its coastal location with a 400-year recorded history of vulnerability to the effects of tsunami in turn generated by seismic activity.

The high risks and vulnerability of nuclear power plants in geologically unstable zones was always a concern of the Japanese public. As I wrote in 2007, such anxieties were dramatically highlighted by the impact of an earthquake upon the Kashiwazaki-Kariwa nuclear power plant in Niigata Prefecture on 16 July 2007. Fortified to withstand earthquakes as strong as 6.5 on the Richter scale, the

---

2   Daniel P. Aldrich, *Site Fights: Divisive Facilities and Civil Society in Japan and the West* (Ithaca and London: Cornell University Press, 2008).

plant nevertheless suffered a fire and leakage. In the first four decades of Japan's nuclear power industry, no major quake-linked damage to plants occurred. The fifth decade was another story. During the five or so years prior to the Fukushima disaster, three incidents occurred: at the Onagawa Plant (August 2005); the Shika Plant (March 2007); and the Kashiwazaki Plant. In each case, the maximum ground motion was greater than the design criteria of the plants with respect to seismic activity.[3] Of great public concern and a matter of high scandal, as Japanese scientist Ishibashi Katsuhiko then explained, the enforcement policy was also in 'shambles'.[4]

In the event, the unthinkable happened on 11 March 2011 in the wake of the Richter-level 9 Tohoku earthquake and tsunami of biblical proportions, which led three of the six nuclear reactors at the Fukushima Daiichi Nuclear Power Plant to meltdown. A nuclear accident rivalled only by Chernobyl, the Fukushima disaster arguably has generated as much international as local attention, at least as to nuclear issues writ large. That is not to belittle local impacts including radiation exposure to residents and clean-up workers, eerily reminiscent to the fate of *hibakusha* from 1945. It was simply Japan's biggest disaster since, incredibly, the atomic bombing

3   Geoffrey Gunn, 'Southeast Asia's Looming Nuclear Power Industry,' *Asia-Pacific Journal | Japan Focus* (Vol. 6, Issue 2, No. 0, 1 February 2008). For the broadcast over Radio Australia (18 January 2012), see www.radioaustralia.net.au/international/radio/onairhighlights/cambodia-joins-queue-for-nuclear-power

4   Ishibashi Katsuhiko, 'Why Worry? Japan's Nuclear Plants at Grave Risk From Quake Damage,' *The Asia-Pacific Journal | Japan Focus* (Vol. 5, Issue 8, No. 1 August 2007).

of Nagasaki. It may also prove to be the world's largest or most costly industrial accident. In the words of former Prime Minister Kan Naoto (June 2010–August 2011), reflecting upon the worst-case scenario that almost came to pass,

> Up until the accident at the Fukushima reactor, I too was confident that since Japanese technology is of high quality, no Chernobyl-like event was possible . . . when I came face to face with Fukushima, I learned I was completely mistaken. I learned first and foremost that we stood on the brink of disaster: had the incident spread only slightly, half the territory of Japan, half the area of metropolitan Tokyo would have been irradiated and 50,000,000 people would have had to evacuate.

It was a wake-up call heard around the world with much international sympathy and support for the victims, including the United States providing crucial technical support and human resources in a high-risk environment, and with the nationals of many countries evacuating their citizens. Internationally, Italy, Germany and Switzerland reversed their civilian nuclear power projection plans. Even China submitted its nuclear power plants to stress checks. Taiwan called for a halt, while Indonesia and Vietnam rethought their plans. Domestically, the nation was stunned – and not a little fearful. Opposition mounted across Japan to nuclear power as citizens started to count the cost and as even former prime ministers began to reveal the full dimension of the crisis. Incredibly though, as explained by Jeff Kingston, 'the institutional and individual pro-nuclear advocates who comprise the utilities, nuclear vendors, bureaucracy, Diet, financial sector, media and academia' – collectively Japan's 'nuclear village' – launched its pushback, not without a great deal of disinformation and outright lies as it sought to override massive negative public opinion.

How did nuclear-averse Japan arrive at its Fukushima moment? 'Atoms for Peace' was the title of a speech delivered by US President Dwight D. Eisenhower to the UN General Assembly on 8 December 1953. Eisenhower's speech opened a media campaign that would last for years. It aimed at 'emotion management', balancing fears of continuing nuclear armament with promises of peaceful use of uranium in future nuclear reactors. The speech was a tipping point for international focus on peaceful uses of atomic energy, even during the early stages of the Cold War. However, recent historians have tended to see the speech as a Cold War manoeuver directed primarily at US allies in Europe. Eisenhower wanted to make sure that the European allies would go along with the shift in NATO strategy from an emphasis on conventional weapons to cheaper nuclear weapons.

According to Peter Kuznick, when the US Information Service (USIS) and the CIA launched their vigorous campaign to promote nuclear energy in Japan, they turned to Shoriki Matsutaro who ran the right-of-centre *Yomiuri Shimbun* newspaper and the Nippon Television Network. Released without trial after two years' imprisonment as a Class-A war criminal, Shoriki's virulent anti-communism evidently redeemed him in American eyes. Surrounded by much hype and ceremony, on 1 November 1955, the *Yomiuri* co-sponsored a US exhibit welcoming the atom back to Japan.

More generally, USIS and other US agencies launched a major campaign to promote and socialize Eisenhower's 'atoms for peace agenda', not only to neutralize the anti-nuclear allergy internationally but to actually sell its reactors. In 1954, the Japanese government began funding its own nuclear research program. In December 1955, it passed the Atomic Energy Basic Law, establishing the Japan Atomic Energy Commission (JAEC), as the body which sets the nation's nuclear policy. Japan purchased its first commercial reactor from Britain but quickly switched to US-designed light water reactors. By mid-1957, the government had contracted to buy 20 additional reactors.

But intensified USIS activities over the coming years began to bear fruit. According to Kuznick, a classified report on the US propaganda campaign showed that in 1956, 70 per cent of Japanese equated 'atom' with 'harmful', but the number had dropped to 30 per cent just two years later. Wanting their country to be a modern scientific-industrial power and knowing Japan lacked energy resources, the public allowed itself to be convinced that nuclear power was safe and clean. It had forgotten the lessons of Hiroshima and Nagasaki. Still, to make the civilian nuclear power project feasible, Japan required a reliable source of uranium. This is where Australia enters the picture as supplier down until the present. When entering into negotiations in the early 1970s, Australia virtually made Japan's entry into the NPT regime a precondition for the export of uranium, especially over concerns that Japan could use the material for military purposes.[5] Although Tokyo ratified the NPT in 1976 and the CTBT in 1997, the apprehension still remains.

5   National Archives of Australia (NAA) A5908, 454.

Prior to the Fukushima disaster, Japan generated 30 per cent of its power from nuclear energy and was planning to expand that to 40 per cent. It had 54 plants in operation, two under construction with 10 more planned. Significant amounts of reactor-grade plutonium are created as a by-product of the nuclear energy industry. Japan was reported in 2012 to have 9 tonnes of plutonium in situ, enough for more than 1,000 nuclear warheads, and an additional 35 tonnes stored in Europe. More than that, as Japan specialist Gavan McCormack commented in 2007, Japan was positioning itself as a 'plutonium superpower' that would go beyond its status as the world's most committed nuclear country to celebrating itself as 'nuclear obsessed'. By this it is meant that, alone among non-nuclear weapon states, Japan pursued the full nuclear cycle in which plutonium is used as fuel after the reprocessing of spent reactor waste, just as Japan has accumulated more than 45 tonnes of plutonium or almost one-fifth of the global stock of civil plutonium.[6] With such nations as China and Russia voicing their concerns, on 24 March 2014 Japan agreed to a request from Washington to return to the US more than 700 pounds (320 kg) of weapons-grade plutonium and highly enriched uranium earlier granted for research purposes. With growing international criticism at the exception given to Japan to reprocess spent nuclear fuel, the issue resurfaced on 16 July 2018, on the occasion of the extension of the 30-year Japan–US Nuclear Cooperation Agreement.[7]

6   Gavan McCormack, 'Japan as a Plutonium Superpower,' *The Asia-Pacific Journal | Japan Focus* (Vol. 5, Issue 12, No. 9 December 2007).

7   Keisuke Katori and Toshihide Ueda, 'Japan's stockpile of plutonium causes jitters as pact is renewed,' *The Asahi Shimbun* (17 July 2018).

The specter of modern *hibakusha* is spreading. Notwith-standing the Fukushima meltdown disaster, Asia remains the part of the world where civilian nuclear power is growing significantly. According to a report by the pro-industry World Nuclear Association on Asia's nuclear energy growth updated to April 2018, there are about 130 operable nuclear power reactors in Asia, 35 under construction and firm plans to build an additional 70–80. Major growth over the past decade has been in China, boasting 38 operable reactors and with 20 under construction. The figures for India are 22 operable reactors, and with six under construction. For its part, South Korea has 24 operable reactors with four under construction.[8] Among major Pacific Rim countries, only New Zealand and Singapore are without research reactors. Indonesia also decided to either pull out of nuclear energy or cancel development plans in the wake of the Fukushima crisis, and the Philippines had much earlier abandoned a completed but unused plant over fears of seismic risks. In Taiwan, where the anti-nuclear movement far predates the events of 2011, nuclear energy remains highly contested by civilians and politicians alike.

In the aftermath of the Fukushima disaster, all 50 of Japan's nuclear plants were closed or had their operations suspended for safety inspections, with the last going offline on 5 May 2012. Seemingly, Japan's nuclear power development had suffered a crippling blow especially after, in an unprecedented act, three former prime ministers came out in opposition to nuclear power. Still in denial that a technically defined

---

8   World Nuclear Association. Asia's Nuclear Energy Growth (updated April 2018).

'meltdown' even occurred and exercising heavy-handed news censorship, Abe Shinzo's pro-nuclear lobby-backed government has used all means at its disposal to restart idling reactors despite popular discontent. Not even a powerful 7.4 scale aftershock and accompanying tsunami off the coast of Fukushima on 22 November 2016 gave pause, nor the 6 September 2018 earthquake on Hokkaido which left a nuclear power plant reliant upon emergency backup power offering a stark parallel with the out-of-control Fukushima disaster.

In late 2016 the Tokyo government announced plans to decommission the failed Monju prototype fast-breeder reactor project (itself costing hundreds of billions of yen) and to replace it with a demonstration fast reactor. As the *Asahi Shimbun* commented upon this decision, 'Japan is caught between a rock and a hard place when it comes to pressing ahead with its dream of a perpetual energy source through nuclear fuel recycling.' It is still left with a huge stockpile of plutonium and, if weaponized, sufficient to produce thousands of atomic weapons. Neither does the Tokyo government have a credible plan to reduce the stockpile in the coming years. Unlike Monju, which would have used and generated plutonium, a fast reactor only burns plutonium. Despite demonstrable public opposition to restarts of idled reactors, on 14 September 2017 JAEC released a white paper, the first since the 3/11 event, confirming that nuclear power should provide 20 per cent of the Japan's energy mix in 2030. The Tokyo Electric Power Company was endorsed as a reliable contractor. The report also endorsed pursuit of a nuclear fuel cycle program using plutonium despite the decision to scrap the Monju reactor.[9]

9   Mari Yamaguchi, 'Japan commission supports nuclear power despite Fukushima' Associated Press (14 September 2017).

It has amazed some that, notwithstanding disaster at home, Japan has aggressively pushed ahead with plans to export nuclear plants to Southeast Asia. Such a business-as-usual approach took a blow in October 2016, however, when Vietnam cancelled a contract with Russia and a consortium of Japanese firms citing lower demand forecasts, rising costs and, especially, safety concerns. The facility, a 4 x 1,000 MW site in the exposed central-south coastal region of Ninh Thuan to have been constructed by International Nuclear Energy Development of Japan (JINED), would have been the first in Southeast Asia. Japan's trade ministry had agreed to finance up to 85 per cent of the total cost.[10]

Writing in 2008 about Japan's then ambitions to outbid South Korea and other countries that sought to sell nuclear power technology to Southeast Asian nations, some with seismic risks and others without technical oversight, I noted that when scientists and engineers get it wrong in the world's most advanced economies, the potential for error or mishap in less advanced is magnified. A Javanese or Vietnamese Chernobyl or even Kashiwazaki is, or should be, unthinkable.

Nagasaki Prefecture does not host a nuclear reactor, but neighbouring prefectures do. Despite official assurances of no abnormalities at nuclear power plants in Kyushu and nearby areas after a series of earthquakes rocked the region in April 2016, calls in and outside of Japan mounted to shut down two newly reopened reactors at the Sendai plant in Kagoshima Prefecture, partly in response to reports that in

---

10 Deutsche Welle News, 'News Vietnam ditches nuclear power plans,' 10 November 2016.

a single month, the Meteorological Agency had recorded nearly 530 quakes at level 1 or above on the Japanese seismic intensity scale in both Kumamoto (contiguous with Nagasaki) and Oita Prefectures, and more than 80 registering 4 or higher on the scale.) During the month, an online Japanese and English-language petition to shut down the Sendai plant drew over 42,000 signatures. In Saga Prefecture, also on Kyushu, some 100 mayors and town heads belonging to the Mayors for a Nuclear Power Free Japan added their voices, calling for the central government and the National Regulation Authority (NRA) to re-evaluate the way earthquake safety standards for nuclear power plants are calculated.[11]

Although the Hiroshima Peace Institute (HPI) was established on 1 April 1998, it would take 14 more years before Nagasaki University launched its Research Center for Nuclear Weapons Abolition (RECNA). In October 2012, Nagasaki Prefecture, City and University came together to establish a Council for Nuclear Weapons Abolition (PCU-NC) as a new framework to work towards a world free from nuclear weapons. As adverted on its website, RECNA is the first such organization in Japan to declare nuclear weapons abolition as its program. Specifically, it seeks, through research, 'to redefine the significance of Hiroshima and Nagasaki experiences in the light of the current world trend, and disseminate information and make proposals from various aspects towards abolishing nuclear weapons', as well as 'to contribute to university education.' Currently headed

11 Eric Johnson, 'Despite assurances, quakes prompt calls to switch off Japan's nuclear reactors' *The Japan Times* (18 April 2016).

by Suzuki Tatsujiro, a nuclear engineer and former vice chairman of the government's Nuclear Energy Commission, RECNA defines itself as a think tank open to the local community longing for nuclear weapons abolition.

Reflection

As the Hiroshima and Nagasaki atomic bombings together starkly symbolized to humankind back in the summer of 1945, the genie was out of the bottle in a nuclear world. With North Korea but the most recent de facto entrant to the nuclear club comprising the United States, Britain, Russia, China, France, India, Israel and Pakistan, Nagasaki City Hall's pitch for nuclear non-proliferation obviously is an ongoing campaign. As this essay has revealed, we cannot ignore the tension besetting Idealists-Globalists and Nationalists-Realists in the framing of the Nagasaki Peace discourse. Primarily, we see a clash between Idealists-Globalists (Nagasaki City Hall), especially in pushing denuclearization and global adherence to the non-Proliferation Treaty, and Realists/Nationalists (Tokyo) waving the banner of the Japan–US Alliance and raising existential threats to Japanese security by nuclear-armed neighbours as an (unstated) rationale for the maintenance of both alliance politics and home-grown nuclear options. In their call for collective defence (read 'rearmament'), the Realists subscribe to the notion of making Japan a 'normal' nation by abandoning the Peace Clause in the Constitution. The spiralling costs associated with the Fukushima clean-up and the decommissioning of other reactors notwithstanding, pushback by Japan's 'nuclear village' can be taken for granted. Whereas the nuclear industry could once tout civilian nuclear power as an alternative to fossil fuel, today in Japan the development of renewable energy has gained widespread acceptance.

On the fringes of the debate stand Japan's neo-nationalists, including those who tried to assassinate Mayor Motoshima. But even within the political mainstream – that is setting aside the largely pacifist, Buddhist-oriented Komeito Party – the ruling Liberal Democratic Party has taken the lead in calling for revision of the Japanese Constitution. They are committed to civilian nuclear power just as the nuclear village circles its wagons. They also understand the military application of the nuclear cycle that produces the plutonium necessary for the production of nuclear weapons, just as some of them stand for an independent Japanese nuclear option.

Obviously Japan's touted peace diplomacy has also shifted over the decades with the Nagasaki and Hiroshima versions of a nuclear-free world jarring with the Tokyo government's refusal to sign off on the UN Treaty on the Prohibition of Nuclear Weapons. To the alarm of many citizens, the concerted push by governments of the day to make Japan a 'normal' country by redefining the role of its armed forces away from a purely defensive role such as suggested by the euphemistic Self-Defense Forces, threatens to vitiate Japan's post-war 'peace constitution'. The Nagasaki and associated Hiroshima peace discourse stands on high moral ground, but anniversaries of the bombings are also exploited nationally as with the procession of politicians to the ignominious sites of nuclear destruction and with some weeping crocodile tears. Together, Hiroshima and Nagasaki have become politically contested sites such as suggested by the visit to Peace Park in Nagasaki on

10 December 2013 by then US Ambassador to Japan, Caroline Kennedy, the 27 May 2016 visit to Hiroshima by US President Barack Obama and the first by a sitting US president, and the August visits to Nagasaki by the Japanese prime minister in 2017 and 2018 and even the (welcome) visit by the UN Secretary-General. But a weary public made even more leery of 'atoms for peace' civilian nuclear power, has responded to the Fukushima debacle with its own war cry, 'No more *hibakusha*', further stretching the meaning of this term and conjuring up a new post-truth narrative firmly embedded in the public space. Long in the shadow of Hiroshima as the first A-bombed city, Nagasaki's appeal to the world as the last city to be so devastated is all the more poignant.

We should be alert as well that the current drive by the Japanese political establishment to remilitarize (and to revise the 'peace' constitution) has gained new momentum and that the unthinkables of the post-war order are now part of the conversation. For sure, this is the Realist position such as struck by the LDP government under Prime Minister Abe just as the Nagasaki peace discourse has been associated in this book with the Idealist/Globalist position (albeit allowing for LDP pressure on Nagasaki). It is also true that the election of Donald Trump as the 45th president of the United States has changed the discourse on nuclear weapons. In particular, as with his invocation to rain down 'fire and fury', on the Korean peninsula, he has added disturbing evidence that the post-war nuclear taboo as a deeply held norm could indeed be challenged by the presidential use of nuclear weapons in the crucible of war.[1] The North Korea detonation of a hydrogen

---

1   Sagan and Valentino, 'Revisiting Hiroshima in Iran,' 79.

bomb on 3 September 2017 along with missile launches over northern Japan have also stoked proponents of a Japanese defence build-up as with the purchase of missile shields, nuclear power plant start-ups, and – although not spoken out loud – even the acquisition of an independent nuclear capability. The Nationalists are now on a roll. Even the stunning LDP electoral victory in the midst of the missile crisis of October 2017 can in large part be credited to popular paranoia over North Korea. Taking due cognizance, on 25 January 2018 the *Bulletin of the Atomic Scientists* pushed its famous Doomsday Clock to 2 minutes before midnight. This was the closest to the apocalypse it has been since 1953, the year when the US and the Soviet Union both tested hydrogen bombs.

Bibliography

Aldrich, Daniel P. (2008) *Site Fights: Divisive Facilities and Civil Society in Japan and the West*. Ithaca and London: Cornell University Press.

Alperovitz, Gar (1965) *The History of the Decision to Use the Atomic Bomb*. New York: Vintage.

—— (1995) *The Decision to Use the Atomic Bomb*. New York: Vintage.

Arima, Tetsuo (2006) 'Shoriki's Campaign to Promote Nuclear Power in Japan and CIA Psychological Warfare' (unpublished paper presented at Tokyo University of Economics, 25 November).

Boxer, Charles (1951) *The Christian Century in Japan, 1549–1650*. Berkeley: University of California Press.

—— (1963) *The Great Ship from Amacon: Annals of Macao and the Old Japan Trade, 1555–1640*. Lisbon: Centro de Estudos Historicos Ultramarinos.
(The best source on early Nagasaki history in the English language remains the classic works of this historian, works cited being good examples.)

Broderick, Mick and David Palmer (2015), 'Australian, British, Dutch and U.S. POWs: Living under the shadow of the Nagasaki Bomb', *The Asia-Pacific Journal | Japan Focus*, Vol. 13, Issue 32, No. 4, 10 August.

Burr, William (ed., 2005) The Atomic Bomb and the End of World War II: A Collection of Primary Sources, National Security Archive Electronic Briefing Book No. 162, 5 August.

Burchett, Wilfred (1946) *Democracy with a Tommygun*. Melbourne and London: F. W Cheshire. Quoted material from pp. 261–91.

—— (1983) *Shadows of Hiroshima*. London: Verso. Quoted material from pp. 44–45.

Burke-Gaffney, Brian (1993) *Nagasaki Speaks: A Record of the Atomic Bombing*. Nagasaki: The Nagasaki International Culture Hall.

—— (2009) *Nagasaki: The British Experience, 1854–1945*. Folkstone: Global Oriental. Quoted material from pp. 91–82.

Buruma, Ian (1994) *The Wages of Guilt: Memories of War in Germany and Japan*. New York: Farrar Straus Giroux. Quoted material from p. 249.

Capodici Vincenzo (interview, 2016); introduction by Shaun Burnie; translation by Richard Minear, 'Reassessing the 3.11 Disaster and the Future of Nuclear Power in Japan: An Interview with Former Prime Minister Kan Naoto', *The Asia-Pacific Journal | Japan Focus*, Vol. 14, Issue 18, No. 1, 15 September. See apjjf.org/2016/18/Capodici.html.

Collie, Craig (2007) *Nagasaki: The Massacre of the Innocent and Unknowing*. Sydney: Allen & Unwin.

Covert, Bryan (1991) 'The Conscience of Japan', *Kyoto Journal*, Spring. See www.inochi-life.net/archives_motoshima_inter-view.html.

Diehl, Chad R. (2008) *Resurrecting Nagasaki – Reconstruction and the Formation of Atomic Narratives*. Ithaca, NY: Cornell University Press. Quoted material from pp. 2, 34–39, 101–02, 117.

Field, Norma (1993) *In the Realm of Dying Emperor*. New York: Vintage Books, esp. Chap. 3.
(*Inter alia*, Field weaves together a string of first-person letter narratives by mostly elderly Nagasaki residents especially responding to Motoshima's position.)

Franklin, H. Bruce (2014) 'Hiroshima, Nagasaki, and American Militarism', *LA Review of Books,* 3 August. See v2..lareviewof-books.org//article/hiroshima-nagasaki-american-militarism.

Goto, Ken'ichi (2003) *Tensions of Empire: Japan and Southeast Asia in the Colonial and Postcolonial World.* Athens: Ohio University Press. Quoted material from p. 291.

Gunn, Geoffrey (2008) 'Southeast Asia's Looming Nuclear Power Industry', *The Asia-Pacific Journal | Japan Focus*, Vol. 6, Issue 2, 1 February. See apjjf.org/-Geoffrey-Gunn/2659/article.html.

—— (2018) *World Trade Systems of the East and West: Nagasaki and the Asian Bullion Trade Networks.* Leiden: Brill.

Ham, Paul (2014) *Hiroshima Nagasaki: The Real Story of the Atomic Bombings and Their Aftermath.* London: Macmillan. Quoted material from p. 474; epilogue.

Havens, Thomas R. H. (1987) *Fire Across the Sea: The Vietnam War and Japan 1965–1975.* Princeton, NJ: Princeton University Press. Quoted material from p.146.

Hein, Laura and Kiko Takenaka (2007) 'Exhibiting World War II in Japan and the United States, *The Asia-Pacific Journal | Japan Focus*, Vol. 5, Issue 7, 3 July. See apjjf.org/-Laura-Hein/2477/article.html.

Hersey, John (1946) 'A Reporter at large, Hiroshima', *The New Yorker*, 31 August 1946.

—— (1946) *Hiroshima,* New York: Alfred A. Knopf. Inc.

Johnson, Bob (2016) *A Doctor's Sword – How an Irish Doctor Survived War, Captivity and the Atomic Bomb.* Cork: Collins Press.

Jordan, Bertrand A. (2016) 'The Hiroshima/Nagasaki Survivor Studies: Discrepancies Between Results and General Perception', *Genetics*, Vol. 203, No. 4. See www.ncbi.nlm.nih.gov/pmc/articles/PMC4981260/. Quoted material on the science surrounding residual radiation effects upon survivors is from pp. 1505–12.

Katsuhiko, Ishibashi (2007) 'Why Worry? Japan's Nuclear Plants at Grave Risk From Quake Damage', *The Asia-Pacific Journal |*

Japan Focus, Vol. 5, Issue 8, 1 August. See apjjf.org/-Ishibashi-Katsuhiko/2495/article.html.

Kingston, Jeff (2012) 'Japan's Nuclear Village', *The Asia-Pacific Journal | Japan Focus*, Vol.10, Issue 37, No.1, 9 September. See apjjf.org/2012/10/37/Jeff-Kingston/3822/article.html.

Kazuyo, Yamane (2006) 'Controversial Exhibitions at Peace Museums in Japan', *Ritsumeikan Kokusai-kenkyu*, Vol. 18, No. 3, March. Quoted material from pp. 473–86.

Kuznick, Peter (2011) 'Japan's nuclear history in perspective: Eisenhower and atoms for war and peace', *Bulletin of the Atomic Scientists*, 13 April.

LeRoy, George V. (1951) *Medical Effects of Atomic Bombs. The Report of the Joint Commission for the Investigation of the Effects of the Atomic Bomb in Japan*; Volume 1, Section 3N, U.S. Atomic Energy Commission. Quoted material from pp.196, 189.

McCormack, Gavan (2007) 'Japan as a Plutonium Superpower', *The Asia-Pacific Journal | Japan Focus*, Vol. 5, Issue 12, 9 December. See apjjf.org/-Gavan-McCormack/2602/article.html.

McCormack, Gavan (2016) 'Japan: Prime Minister Abe Shinzo's Agenda', *The Asia-Pacific Journal | Japan Focus*, Vol. 14, Issue 24, No. 1, 15 December. See apjjf.org/2016/24/McCormack.html.

Miyamoto, Yuki (2012) *Beyond the Mushroom Cloud: Commemoration, Religion, and Responsibility After Hiroshima*. New York: Fordham University. Quoted material from p. 7, 83, chap. 4 *passim*.

Mochizuki, Mike M. and Deepa M. Ollapally, (eds, 2016) *Nuclear Debates in Asia: The Role of Geopolitics and Domestic Processes*. Lanham, MA: Rowman & Littlefield. Quoted material from pp. 6; 12.

The Nagasaki Atomic Bomb Damage Records: General Analysis Version, Vol. I (revised version) (Nagasaki City, 2016, 65–70) which reproduces the 'Atomic Bombing Order' or letter from

General Thomas Handy, Acting Chief of Staff, to General Carl Spaatz of the US Army Strategic Air Force, authorizing the dropping of the first atomic bomb. See www.peace-nagasaki.go.jp/abombrecords/b030405.html.

The Nagasaki Atomic Bomb Damage Records, Part 1, Chap. 2. Nagasaki National Peace Memorial Hall for the Atomic Bomb Victims.

Otsuki, Tomoe (2015) 'The Politics of Reconstruction and Reconciliation in U.S-Japan Relations—Dismantling the Atomic Bomb Ruins of Nagasaki's Urakami Cathedral', *The Asia-Pacific Journal | Japan Focus*, Vol.13, Issue 32, No. 2, 10 August. See apjjf.org/2015/13/32/Tomoe-Otsuki/4356.html.

Putnam, Frank W. (1998) 'The Atomic Bomb Casualty Commission in retrospect', *Proceedings of the National Academy of Sciences of the United States of America*. PNAS, Vol. 95. No.10. Quoted material from pp. 5426–31.

Sagan, Scott D. and Benjamin A. Valentino (2017) 'Revisiting Hiroshima in Iran: What Americans Really Think about Using Nuclear Weapons and Killing Noncombatants', *International Security*, Vol. 42, Issue 1. Quoted material from pp. 79, 486

Schäfer, René (1985) *Terug naar Fukuoka 14, krijgsgevangene in Nagasaki* (Back to Fukuoka, prisoner of war in Nagasaki). Amsterdam: Verschenen.

—— (1983) *Oranda heishi nagasaki hibakuki*. Tokyo: Sodo Bunka.

Selden, Kyoko and Mark Selden (eds, 1989) *The Atomic Bomb – Voices from Hiroshima and Nagasaki*. New York: M.E. Sharpe. Quoted material from pp. xxiv, xvii.

Selden, Mark (2016) 'American Fire Bombing and Atomic Bombing of Japan in History and Memory', *The Asia-Pacific Journal | Japan Focus*, Vol.14, Issue 23, 1 December. See apjjf.org/2016/23/Selden.html.

Southard, Susan (2015) *Nagasaki Life After Nuclear War*. New York: Viking. Quoted material from pp. 222–23, 349–72.

Stellingwerff, Johannes (1980) *Nederlandse Krijgsgevangenen overleven de Atoombom*. Franeker, Uitgevrij Wever.

Sweeney, Charles W., with James A. Antonucci and Marion K. Antonucci (1997), *War's End: An Eyewitness Account of America's Last Atomic Mission*. New York: Avon Books.

Takeshi, Nagai (ed., 1951) *We of Nagasaki: The Story of Survivors in an Atomic Wasteland*. London: Victor Gollancz Ltd.

Takeshi, Nagai (1984) *The Bells of Nagasaki* (trans. William Johnston). Tokyo: Kodansha International.

Takeshi, Nagai (2008) *Leaving My Beloved Children Behind* (trans. Maurice M. Tatsuoka and Tsuneyoshi Takai). Australia: St. Pauls Publications.

Tanter, Richard (1987) 'Voice and Silence in the First Nuclear War: Wilfred Burchett and Hiroshima', in Ben Kiernan (ed.) *Burchett Reporting the Other Side of the World, 1939–1983*. London: Quartet Books. Quoted material from pp. 18–21.

Tibbets, Paul W. (1982) *The Tibbets' Story*. New York: Stein & Day. Quoted material taken from Chap. 32, 'End of the War', p. 240.

Urquhart, Alistair (2010) *The Forgotten Highlander: My Incredible Story of Survival During the War in the Far East*. Brattleboro, VT: Skyhorse.

US War Department, Magic Diplomatic Summary, no. 1214, 22 July 1946.

Warner, Denis (1995) 'They saw the Fat Man and lived to tell the tale', *The Australian Magazine,* 1–2 July, pp. 51–55.

Weller, George (2007) 'First into Nagasaki: George Weller's Censored Eyewitness Dispatches on the atomic bombing and Japan's POWs', *The Asia-Pacific Journal | Japan Focus*, Vol. 5, Issue 1, 2 January. See apjjf.org/-Anthony-Weller/2330/article.html.

Weller, George and Anthony Weller (ed., 2006) *First into Nagasaki: The Censored Eyewitness Dispatches on Post-Atomic Japan and Its Prisoners of War*. New York: Crown.

Winkler, Dolf (2002) *Mijn kampverleden 1942–1945* (My Past Camp 1942–1945), Emmeloord: Drukwinkel Emmeloord B.V.

Zohar, Ayelet (2016) 'Images of Hiroshima', in David P. Chandler, Robert Cribb and Li Narangoa, (eds) *End of Empire: 100 Days in 1945 That Changed Asia and the World*. Copenhagen: NIAS Press, pp. 41–42.

Websites

Democracy Now
· Weller, Anthony [interviewed by Amy Goodman] 'Long-Suppressed Nagasaki Article Discovered.' 5 August 2005. See www.democracynow.org/2005/8/5/long__suppressed_nagasaki_article_discovered.

Federation of American Scientists, 'Nuclear Weapons Program.' See fas.org/issues/nuclear-weapons/status-world-nuclear-forces/.

Gunn, Geoffrey, Interview with Radio Australia, 18 January 2012. See www.radioaustralia.net.au/international/radio/onairhighlights/cambodia-joins-queue-for-nuclear-power

Huffington Post
· Mitchell, Greg (2011) 'For 64th Anniversary: The Great Hiroshima Cover-Up – And the Nuclear Fallout for All of Us Today'. The Blog, 25 May, See www.huffingtonpost.com/greg-mitchell/for-64th-anniversary-the_b_252752.html

MIT Visualizing Cultures
· Dower, John 'Ground Zero 1945: Pictures by Atomic Bomb Survivors', See visualizingcultures.mit.edu/groundzero1945/index.html

National Security Archive. nsarchive.gwu.edu/
Among the photos released by the Archive in 2016 are depictions of Air Force operations in Okinawa, including little-known pictures of US nuclear bombs deployed there during the 1960s. Documents posted by the Archive about 'Operation Crossroads' shed light on the Lucky Dragon incident as do galleries of declassified videos and photographs. Of two tests staged to determine the effects of the new weapons on warships, the 'Baker test' was the most dangerous by contaminating nearby test ships with radioactive mist.

National Archives of Australia (NAA) www.naa.gov.au/
Australian archives sources are more specific as to POW recovery.

· (NAA) B3856, 140/11/3394 Prisoners of War recovered from Nagasaki, Japan – Includes a Nominal Roll, dated October 1945. Besides the ABCD group, they included Norwegians, South Africans, Czech, Portuguese, West Indians, 'Malays' and 'Arabs', and with 127 unaccounted for at the time of evacuation.

· (NAA) A462 449/2 Part 3.

Nagasaki National Peace Memorial Hall for the Atomic Bomb Victims. See: www.peace-nagasaki.go.jp/en/

Oka Masaharu Nagasaki Peace Museum. See: www.d3.dion.ne.jp/~okakinen [9-4 Nishizaka-machi, Nagasaki, 850-0051. tel. 095-820-5600].

· Peace Monuments, '26 Monuments Related to Nagasaki: But Not In Nagasaki (Japan)'. See peace.maripo.com/p_nagasaki.htm.

POW Research Network Japan. www.powresearch.jp/en/

· Fukubayashi, Toru 'POW Camps in Japan Proper POW Research Network Japan.'

Research Center for Nuclear Weapons Abolition, Nagasaki University (RECNA). www.recna.nagasaki-u.ac.jp/recna/en-top

U.S. National Archives www.archives.gov/

· Record Group 77, Records of the Office of the Chief of Engineers, Manhattan Engineer District, TS Manhattan Project File '42-'46, folder 5D Selection of Targets, 2 Notes on Initial Meeting of Target Committee, 2 May 1945, Source: RG 77, MED Records, Top Secret Documents, File no. 5d.

World Nuclear Association. Asia's Nuclear Energy Growth (updated April 2018). www.world-nuclear.org/information-library/country-profiles/others/asias-nuclear-energy-growth.aspx

Newspapers and News Services

AsiaNews.it, including quoted material from:
· 'Nagasaki mayor calls for a nuclear-free world', 8 September 2012.

Associated Press, including quoted material from:
· Mari Yamaguchi, 'Japan commission supports nuclear power despite Fukushima', 14 September 2017.

Akahata, including quoted material from:
· 'Sasebo residents protest against U.S. nuclear-powered aircraft carrier's visit', 1 & 2 March 2009.
· 'High court overturns order to pay benefits to South Korean Hibakusha', 23 January 2007.

Russia Behind the Headlines (RBTH), including quoted material from:
· Sinelschikova, Yekaterina, 'International tribunal should prosecute perpetrators of Hiroshima, Nagasaki bombings', 6 August 2015.

The Asahi Shimbun, including quoted material from:
· 'Japan Catholics to get photo of Nagasaki boy signed by pope', 25 July 2018.
· 'Japan unable to scrap recycling program due to plutonium stocks', 1 December 2016.

· Katori, Keisuke and Toshihide Ueda, 'Japan's stockpile of plutonium causes jitters as pact is renewed', 17 July 2018.

· Okada, Shohei 'Nagasaki mayor tells world: Visit to see how
  nukes affect humans', 9 August 2016.

· Takashima, Yosuke and Kentaro Yamano, 'Hiroshima, Nagasaki
  release Soviet footage of A-bomb damage', 5 August 2016.

· Yamano, Kentaro, 'Russian official condemns U.S. A-bombings in
  Nagasaki visit', 4 November 2016.

The Daily Telegraph, including quoted material from:

· Bill Reed, 'Aussie Nagasaki atomic bomb survivor who counted
  his blessings', 5 September 2016.

The Daily Yomiuri, including quoted material from:

· Nagai, Asami 'Making peace with the past. How one small town
  in Kyushu is going out of its way to promote reconciliation
  between former enemies', 29 July 2000.

Deutsche Welle News, including quoted material from:

· 'Gauck pays respects to Nagasaki victims', 18 November 2016.

· 'News Vietnam ditches nuclear power plans', 10 November 2016.

The Independent, including quoted material from:

· Forster, Katie 'Photos of Nagasaki reveal devastating aftermath of
  1945 US atomic bomb',, 23 September 2013.

The Japan Times, including quoted material from:

· Johnson, Eric 'Despite assurances, quakes prompt calls to switch
  off Japan's nuclear reactors', 18 April 2016.

· 'Justice for A-bomb victims overseas', 22 September 2015.

· Kim, Sam 'Hibakusha of "Korea's Hiroshima" still press for
  redress', 6 August 2015.

· McNeil, David, 'Strategic approach: Washington's shifting nuclear
  policy in the Asia-Pacific region is putting Japan in a difficult
  position', 30 July 2017).

· 'Nagasaki A-bomb survivor and victims' advocate Taniguchi dies at 88', 30 August 2017.

· Naryshkiin, 'Putin aide Naryshkin eyes Hiroshima visit in June', 14 April 2016.

· Shintomi, Tetsuo, 'Nagasaki hibakusha recalls struggle to dodge discrimination', 16 March 2015.

Japan Today, including quoted material from:

· 'Nagasaki mayor to refer to Fukushima accident in peace declaration', 29 July 2011.

The Korean Herald, including quoted material from:

· Lee, Joel, 'Nagasaki atom bomb survivor urges denuclearization of world', 25 September 2016.

The Mainichi, including quoted material from:

· Sayo, Kato 'Hibakusha: Arrogance of runaway gov't could lead to war: ex-Nagasaki Univ. pres.', 16 November 2016.

The New York Times, including quoted material from:

· Sanger, David E. 'Special to The New York Times, Mayor Who Faulted Hirohito Is Shot', 19 January 1990.

TASS, including quoted material from

· 'Russia against silencing "ugly moral side" of Japan bombings in 1945, Duma speaker calls for legal assessment of the nuclear bombings of Japanese cities', 4 August 2016.

· 'Russia publishes unique 1945 Soviet embassy report of Hiroshima bombing' by Ilyshev-Vvedensky, 6 August 2015.

Xinhua, including quoted material from:

· 'Nagasaki marks 71st anniv. of A-bombing amid calls for reflecting on Japan's aggression history', 8 September 2016.

Index

censorship, 39, 49–50; government, 26, 28, 35, 38, 66–67;
media, 34–37; navy, 29, 31, 36,
42, 45, 57–58, 60, 105; nuclear
bombings, 70–71; nuclear tests,
47, 105, 108, 119, 122; occupation, 2, 37–38, 47, 50, 58;
Senate, 43–44; war planners, 9,
27. *See also* America
United States Information Service
(USIS), 110–11 *See also*
United States
Urakami, 11, 48, 56, 81; bombed,
19–21; Cathedral, 11,74,
88–90; factory district, 14–15
Urquhart, Alistair, 60

Valentino, Benjamin A., 44
Vietnam, 6, 109, 115; bombing of,
22, 62; Japan invasion of, 68

war, 63–64
war of aggression perspective,
67–69. *See also* China
war crimes, 67–68, 111. *See also*
Japan
War Rescript, 27–28
Warner, Denis, 59
Weller, Anthony, 34, 36, 60
Weller, George, 33–36
Winkler, Dolf, 61–62
World Nuclear Association, 113

Xinhua, 68–70

Yamaguchi-gumi, 96
Yamahata Yosuke, 38–41
Yamane, Kazuyo, 86–87
Yomiuri Shimbun, 110
Yoshida Shigeru (prime minister),
106

ABOUT THE AUTHOR: Geoffrey Gunn is emeritus professor of Nagasaki University. He is a widely written scholar in Asian history, most notably on Indochina, his works including *Monarchical Manipulation in Cambodia* (recently published by NIAS Press). He has also published on the early economic history of Nagasaki and is a contributor to and an editor of T*he Asia-Pacific Journal | Japan Focus* (apjjf.org/). Besides Japan, he has taught in universities in Australia, Libya, Singapore, Brunei and Macau. He lives in Nagasaki.